Created and designed
by the editorial staff
of Ortho Books.

ANNE COOLMAN
Project Editor

CYNTHIA SCHEER
Writer and
Food Stylist

LINDA HINRICHS
Designer

DENNIS GRAY
Photographer

SARA SLAVIN
Photographic
Stylist

Ortho Books

Publisher
Robert L. Iacopi

Editorial Director
Min S. Yee

Managing Editor
Anne Coolman

Horticultural Editor
Michael D. Smith

Senior Editor
Kenneth R. Burke

Production Manager
Laurie Sheldon

Editors
Barbara J. Ferguson
Sally W. Smith

Horticulturists
Michael D. McKinley
Deni W. Stein

Production Assistant
Darcie S. Furlan

Editorial Assistants
Laurie A. Black
Anne D. Pederson
William F. Yusavage

National Sales Manager
Garry P. Wellman

Operations/Distribution
William T. Pletcher

Operations Assistant
Donna M. White

Administrative Assistant
Georgiann Wright

Address all inquiries to:
Ortho Books
Chevron Chemical Company
Consumer Products Division
575 Market Street
San Francisco, CA 94105

First Printing in April, 1983

1 2 3 4 5 6 7 8 9

83 84 85 86 87 88

ISBN 0-89721-012-3

Library of Congress Catalog Card
Number 82-63124

Acknowledgments

Design:
Linda Hinrichs
Jonson Pederson
Hinrichs & Shakery

Photography:
Dennis Gray
Studio, Mindy Goldfein

Photo Stylist:
Sara Slavin

Illustrations:
Ellen Blonder
Mill Valley, CA

Copyediting:
Editcetera
Berkeley, CA

Typography:
CBM Type
Sunnyvale, CA

Color Separations:
Colorscan
Mountain View, CA

Special Thanks to:
Anne Kupper, Williams-Sonoma
San Francisco, CA
Beans & Leaves Coffee and Tea
San Francisco and Belmont, CA
BIA Cordon Bleu
Belmont, CA
Fran Flanagan
San Francisco, CA
Mr. and Mrs. Steve Cooper
Mill Valley, CA
Mr. and Mrs. Robert Johnson
Woodside, CA
Anne McKay
Brooklyn, NY
Karen Usas
Princeton, NJ

Front Cover Photograph

This colorful brunch menu features
Scrambled Eggs in a Crispy Crust
(recipe, page 35), accompanied by
Four Seasons Fresh Fruit Bowl
(recipe, page 22), Spiced Cranberry
Muffins (recipe, page 84), and Italian
Jam-Filled Crescents (recipe, page 93).

Back Cover Photographs

Some of the breakfast and brunch
treats you will find in the pages
ahead are:
Upper left: Sour Cream Coffee Ring,
                 page 85
Upper right: Hot Spiced Cider,
                 page 16
Lower left: Blackberry Cobbler,
                 page 27
Lower right: Parmesan Baked Eggs,
                 page 40

Title Page

Home economist and writer Cynthia
Scheer serves a spring breakfast on
the patio.

Chevron

Chevron Chemical Company
575 Market Street, San Francisco, CA 94105

Breakfast gets your day off to a healthy beginning. Brunch can be less sensible, more fun. Whichever meal whets your appetite, this book is packed with good ideas.

BREAKFASTS & BRUNCHES — THE DAY'S FIRST FOOD

It may be that the world is divided into two groups: those who can hardly wait for the first nourishment of the day and those who can't quite face food until a little later. Either way, this book has something for you: breakfast for the eager or brunch for the slow-to-come-around.

Breakfast gives the early riser a fine foundation for the morning's jobs. Indeed, nutritionists make a convincing case that a healthy breakfast does even more—it keeps you moving efficiently even until the end of the afternoon when lunch is long forgotten.

Brunch, a late-morning meal combining the best elements of breakfast and lunch, is less sensible but more fun. It's an occasion to stretch in the sun, sip wine or something fizzy, and eat delicious things that seem a bit too special for every day.

The festive feeling of brunch makes it a perfect meal situation for entertaining. People don't feel hurried. The concept of the meal is so loose that your menu can define it any way you choose. Depending on your tastes and how much of the food preparation you are willing to do yourself, brunch can also be an economical way to entertain.

A light yet healthy breakfast everyone can enjoy includes fresh fruit, buttered toast, homemade preserves, and coffee or tea with milk. It's colorful, inviting, and boasts a nutritious helping from every food group.

BREAKFAST FOODS

What you eat in the morning may depend on how much time you have and on the eating patterns with which you grew up. Unfortunately, breakfast is often the most rushed meal of the day. That limits some people to a cup of coffee on the run, which is scarcely any breakfast at all. In only a few more minutes, you can augment that with a glass of juice, toast or a muffin, and a bowl of ready-to-eat cereal with milk—making a better balanced repast.

In other parts of the world, breakfast may be the classic Continental combination of coffee and steaming milk, accompanied by freshly baked bread or rolls, lots of butter, and a dollop of fruit preserves or honey. In Germany or Holland, this is often expanded (and made somewhat more satisfying) by adding a wedge of cheese, a soft-cooked egg, or even a slice of sausage.

In Scandinavia, wonderful rye and whole grain breads appear at breakfast, a meal that sometimes becomes a veritable smorgasbord with the addition of cheeses and herring or other fish. The English appear to take the prize for ambitious breakfasts, with hot porridge followed by bacon, sausage, or even kippered herring and grilled tomatoes with eggs.

So it's clear that the foods you choose for breakfast need not become routine. Plenty of variety is available to tempt and nourish you.

A good breakfast doesn't have to be a routine breakfast. The one at left features robust espresso coffee and colorful Breakfast Pizza (the convenient make-ahead recipe is on page 80). If you prefer to ease more gently into the day's activity, select the fare at right: juice and ready-to-eat cereal with fruit and milk.

CHOOSING A NUTRITIOUS BREAKFAST

You hear a lot about eating a "good" breakfast, but it's useful to clarify how food experts define goodness.

In terms of *quantity*, breakfast should account for a fourth to a third of the day's food energy or calories. After all, your body needs fuel to run on during the morning. Consider the meaning of the word breakfast—to break the fast of the night before.

Even if you are counting calories, you are entitled to at least a fourth of the day's allotment at breakfast. It seems that by beginning the day with a satisfying meal, you are less likely to overeat at lunch, dinner, or in-between.

The *quality* of breakfast depends on the food you choose. Black coffee and a sugary doughnut, for example, contain little but carbohydrates, fat, and possibly a few B vitamins. Your body deserves more than that.

Use the Basic Four Food Plan to make nutritious breakfast choices. The groups are (clockwise from upper left): fruits and vegetables, meat and other protein foods, milk and dairy products such as cheese and yogurt, and breads and cereals. Recipe for the Orange-Date Muffins is on page 84.

A simple guide for selecting healthy breakfasts—and other meals, as well—is the division of all foods into the Basic Four Food Plan. The four food groups are: (1) milk and other dairy products, (2) meat and other protein foods (fish, poultry, eggs, cheese, dried peas and beans, and nuts), (3) fruits and vegetables, and (4) breads and cereals.

Nutritionists suggest that for breakfast you include foods from at least three of these four groups. The morning meal is a good time to get the vitamin C (ascorbic acid) you need every day. Good sources include citrus fruits and juices (orange or grapefruit), strawberries, cantaloupe, and tomato juice.

If all this sounds too predictable to you, you are probably the sort of person who would enjoy practically any kind of food for breakfast. And why not! A good breakfast can take many forms.

Leaf through this book and you will find a variety of options: nutritious fruit shakes that make a quick, delicious breakfast-in-a-glass; fresh strawberry shortcake with whipped cream and buttery homemade biscuits; speedy breakfast pizza on broiled English muffins; grilled cheese-and-tomato sandwiches. Each of these includes a nutritionally significant amount of food from each of the four basic groups.

BREAKFAST BASIC: WHAT MAKES A GOOD FRYING PAN?

If breakfast requires any cooking at all, the utensil you probably reach for nine times out of ten is a frying pan. (Maybe you call it a skillet—the two terms are roughly synonymous for a shallow, long-handled cooking pan with sloping sides.)

Whatever you call this utensil, it is useful to know some of the characteristics that enable a frying pan to perform well. The choices in materials and design in today's frying pans can be a little bewildering. If you are in the market for a new one, here are some tips that can help you decide.

Cookware experts say the single most important factor in choosing a good frying pan is its weight. A simple rule is to select the heaviest one you can handle easily. The heavier the pan, the better and more evenly it will hold and conduct heat, and the less likely it is to warp or buckle with long use.

Consider, also, the balance of a prospective frying pan. It should sit evenly on the cooking surface and not be tipped askew by a too-heavy handle. Heft it—the design of the handle should permit you to lift and tilt the pan skillfully.

How well a frying pan conducts heat depends in large part on the substance from which it is made. Copper is the best heat conductor for surface cooking, and a heavy French copper skillet is the first choice of many good cooks. Quality copper pans are esteemed because of their beauty and durability—they last forever and can be handed down to the next generation. And when you cook with copper, you use relatively low heat, saving fuel.

On the minus side, however, copper pans are usually lined with tin, which must be replaced in time. An idea that sounds extravagant—replacing the tin lining with silver—may be practical when one considers the greater durability of silver over the life of the pan. Of course, both copper and silver require frequent polishing to look their best.

Considerably less costly—and with as many partisans as a material for the perfect frying pan—is iron. It is used in two quite different forms: rolled steel is the lighter weight and is often seen in omelet and crêpe pans; cast iron is much heavier, and may be unfinished or coated with porcelain enamel. All forms conduct heat well. Both rolled steel and uncoated cast iron pans must be seasoned often with oil and kept in a dry place to remain rust-free.

To season a pan of this sort, first scrub it with fine steel wool and wash it well. Then coat the inside generously with a flavorless vegetable oil (preferably not safflower oil). Place the pan over medium heat and heat it until the fat begins to smoke. Remove the pan from the heat and let it cool completely, then use paper towels to wipe out the excess oil. Af-

ter seasoning, the pan —especially an omelet pan —should never be washed. Simply wipe it clean with a paper towel and a little oil after use. From time to time, you may need to repeat the seasoning process.

Some enameled cast iron frying pans have a dark, nonstick coating applied by the manufacturer. It is designed for high-temperature cooking. For this and other special finishes, it is a good idea to follow the maker's directions for seasoning or otherwise preparing the pan before using it for cooking. Read the label or accompanying literature.

Cast iron is not as indestructible as its weight might suggest. If dropped on a hard surface, it may crack or break. It is also too heavy for many people to handle without a struggle.

Aluminum is another material that makes a fine frying pan. Aluminum pans come in many forms. Spun aluminum frying pans in classic French shapes, especially omelet pans, are versatile. One can also find a handsome variety of cast aluminum skillets. In all its forms aluminum is a good conductor of heat, but it is rather soft; abrasive cleaners should be used cautiously. Because aluminum is lightweight, it can be used to make a pan that is thick enough to hold heat well, but that is so light that it handles easily.

Special finishes have given aluminum cookware a new lease on life in the past several years. Developed for professional cooks, Calphalon cookware with its smooth, dark, fused-on coating will not discolor or react chemically with food and resists sticking.

A different sort of finish is DuPont's durable new SilverStone nonstick coating, which is fused into the pan material. You will find it on the aluminum frying pans of many manufacturers. Be sure the pan beneath is worthy of the coating. For many years of dependable use, choose a well constructed pan that is substantial enough not to warp.

Finally, there is stainless steel. In spite of its good looks, this material has long had a bad name among serious cooks. Stainless steel is known to be a poor conductor, with hot spots where food sticks or burns. If you insist on using it, look for a stainless steel pan with a bottom containing a thick core of some other metal with better heat-conducting properties —copper or aluminum.

Regardless of the material you select, for all-around breakfast cooking you will probably want frying pans of at least two different sizes. For omelets, experienced cooks say an 8-inch-diameter pan is the most useful. A 10- to 12-inch frying pan is a good size for other preparations —scrambling or frying eggs, sautéeing bacon or sausages, and many others.

Find your favorite skillet. Clockwise from upper left: the pans shown are of Calphalon, SilverStone coating on aluminum, enameled cast iron, cast aluminum, stainless steel, and cast iron. Copper pan is at center.

Enjoy the luxury of a leisurely weekend morning with a breakfast or brunch of Fresh Spinach and Mushroom Omelet (the recipe is on page 38), Cheddar Cheese Muffins (page 84), juice, and milk, tea, or coffee. For a treat, add Orange Bundt Batter Bread (page 91).

For many of us, coffee equals breakfast. But coffee is hardly the whole story. Consider hot chocolate, breakfast tea, and fresh fruit juice blends.

BREAKFAST BEVERAGES, BREWED OR BUBBLING

Waking up to the fragrance of good coffee brewing is one of life's small delights. Even if you are not particularly fond of drinking coffee, its aroma is probably a pleasure. Mingled with morning sunshine, the smell of fine coffee seems to carry the promise of the day's possibilities.

For those who prefer to sip something other than coffee in the morning, the alternatives are many. Frothy hot chocolate is almost as rich in historic associations as is coffee. A well made cup of sturdy breakfast tea has many devotees. Fresh fruit juices, in place of or as an accompaniment to a hot drink, are nutritious eye-openers.

And for brunch, one can begin with the elegance of chilled Champagne or other sparkling wine. From there it is only a step to a creamy gin fizz, a brisk Bloody Mary, or an icy fresh fruit daiquiri foamy from the blender.

Orange juice is such a popular breakfast beverage that it is known by its initials alone. But it's not the whole story. Read on for exciting alternatives—coffee, tea, chocolate, and other juices.

COFFEE

If you judged coffee only by the convincingly enacted scenarios of television commercials, you could easily believe that a great cup of coffee starts with a jar of instant coffee or a vacuum-packed can of ground coffee from the supermarket. But if your taste in coffee is more critical, it's clear that that is only the beginning of the coffee story.

The proliferation of shops specializing in coffees from all over the world attests to a growing interest in fine coffee. Sold as whole beans or ground to order, such coffees are also available in a variety of roasts, in any quantity you like.

If exploring coffee is new to you, you may wish to try just a small amount of several types—say ¼ pound. When you find your favorite, then purchase a larger quantity. The

A French breakfast depends on the bracing nourishment of strong coffee mixed liberally with hot milk. You will find more about the elegant porcelain pot on page 12. A recipe for the homemade Strawberry-Rhubarb Preserves is on page 94.

flavor of coffee is affected in part by its origin: coffee-producing areas include high-altitude regions of several South American and African nations.

Roasting develops the flavor of coffee and determines the darkness and shininess of the beans. Darker roasts are popular for after-dinner coffee and for breakfast coffee that will be mixed with a quantity of hot milk. Of these, Vienna roast is the lightest, and French and Italian, or espresso, *roast are the darkest.*

Freshness is one of the most critical factors in brewing a fine cup of coffee. Ground coffee loses flavor quickly, and that is why many connoisseurs buy whole coffee beans and grind them just before brewing each pot. Store coffee, tightly covered, in a dark, cool place. If you buy coffee in large amounts, package the bulk of it airtight and store it in the freezer. Then remove small amounts as needed. The usual proportion is 2 tablespoons ground coffee for each 8-ounce cup.

The method of brewing is also important. Most experts favor a filter-type drip pot because it removes the brewed coffee fairly quickly from the grounds, and because the coffee can be made with water just below the boiling point—overly high heat is the enemy of good coffee flavor. The French have a saying, "Café bouilli, café foutu" (if it boils, it's killed).

And, of course, the pot should be sparkling clean: any residue of oily coffee film lingering in the pot may contribute an unpleasant flavor. Unusual coffee pots for making special kinds of coffee are discussed on page 12.

SPECIAL POTS FOR SPECIAL COFFEE

If you really enjoy fine coffee, the day will come when your standard, everyday coffee maker is no longer enough. One can virtually tour the world of coffee-appreciating countries through their coffeepots. Here are some of the more interesting-looking varieties.

The Turkish or middle-Eastern ibrik *represents one of the earliest ways of brewing coffee. After all, it comes from the land where coffee was first drunk. Often made of gleaming copper trimmed with brass, it looks like an oversize butter warmer. (Its shape resembles a bell, open at the top.) Making coffee in an* ibrik *is quite unsophisticated—one just pours boiling water over very finely ground dark-roast coffee and stirs until it reaches the desired strength. Some people describe coffee of this type as being so strong it is actually* thick. *It is usually heavily sweetened.*

From France comes the idea of the plunger-type coffeepot *or* cafetière. *It consists of a clear glass carafe that is fitted into a metal or plastic frame. To use it, place finely ground dark-roast coffee in the bottom, and pour in boiling water to the top of the frame. Let the mixture stand to infuse for about 5 minutes, then insert the snug-fitting plunger and slowly press the mesh screen filter down to the bottom. This separates the coffee from the grounds, and it is ready to drink.*

Another good-looking French pot is the three-part porcelain drip coffee maker. *It works much like other drip pots—coarsely ground coffee is placed in the upper portion, and hot water is poured through to drip into the lower part. You will find this style in plain white porcelain or in various patterns that match dinnerware and ovenproof serving dishes.*

Italy is renowned for espresso, *coffee brewed with steam. Although many costly electric espresso makers are available, less expensive stove-top espresso pots also produce a fairly authentic demitasse cup of the dark, fragrant brew.*

The simplest espresso pot is a three-piece, hourglass-shaped affair of polished or satin-finish aluminum. Water goes in the lower pot, finely ground coffee in a basket in the middle. When the water boils, steam rises through the coffee and condenses in the upper container, where the pouring spout is located. When the coffee is ready, it is poured from the top part of the pot.

A more elaborate version of the espresso pot consists of side-by-side containers connected by a hollow overhead bridge. Water is placed in one side, coffee in a basket over an empty metal pitcher on the other. The principle is similar to that of the hourglass-shaped pot: as the water boils, steam is forced through the coffee—hissing all the while—to condense in the pitcher. Some espresso makers of this type also have a jet that, when opened, emits steam that can be used to heat milk for cappuccino.

Another style of Italian coffeepot is a three-piece, drip-filter arrangement that stacks to make a tall cylinder with handles. It is called a macchinetta *or* napoletana. *One places water in the bottom pot and coffee in the perforated filter basket in the center. When the water boils, the pot is turned over, and the water drips through the coffee into the empty container with the pouring spout.*

CAFE AU LAIT

Breakfast in France has more substance than one might think, thanks to the amount of rich, steaming milk that is poured into those oversize coffee cups in which *cafe au lait* is served. It may be the flakiness of the croissant that you remember, but it's the protein of the milk that keeps you going until restaurants open for lunch at half-past noon.

> **1 cup milk**
> **2 cups strong, hot, dark-roast coffee**
> **Sugar (optional)**

1. Pour milk into a small saucepan. Place over medium heat until milk is steaming hot but just under the boiling point. Pour into a warm pitcher.

2. Fill large coffee cups or mugs two-thirds full of hot coffee. Add hot milk, stirring to blend. Add sugar to taste.

Makes 2 to 3 servings.

CAFFÈ LATTE

The Italian interpretation of *café au lait* is made with hot milk frothy with steam created by an espresso pot with a steam jet—sometimes called a *cappuccino* pot. The only real difference between *caffe latte* and cappuccino is the size of the cup; cappuccino is served in a smaller one.

> **2 cups milk**
> **2 cups hot espresso coffee**
> **Ground cinnamon or powdered, sweetened cocoa**
> **Sugar (optional)**

1. Using steam from an espresso coffee maker, heat milk in a deep, heatproof container until frothy. Pour most of the milk, reserving a little of the foam, into 4 tall, heatproof mugs.

2. Slowly pour coffee down sides of mugs. Spoon reserved milk foam over coffee. Sprinkle lightly with cinnamon or cocoa.

3. Serve with spoons. Add sugar to taste.

Makes 4 servings.

IRISH COFFEE

Too rich for all but the most opulent breakfasts, Irish coffee might be served as a sort of dessert-in-a-glass to cap a winter brunch.

8 sugar lumps (½-in. square)
3 cups strong, hot coffee
6 ounces (¾ cup) Irish whiskey
    Slightly whipped cream

1. Rinse 4 heatproof 8-ounce footed glasses or mugs with hot water and drain quickly.

2. Place 2 lumps sugar in each glass. Add ¾ cup steaming hot coffee and 1½ ounces (3 tablespoons) Irish whiskey to each. Stir well to dissolve sugar.

3. Top each with a dollop of cream and serve at once.

Makes 4 servings.

BREAKFAST TEA

A fine pot of tea in the morning has many enthusiasts. Browse among the teas your favorite coffee-and-tea shop sells, and you will find some designated "breakfast tea," both English and Irish. (The English is usually heartier in flavor.) But any medium- to rich-bodied blend of black tea you enjoy can hit the spot in the morning.

Making a good cup of tea requires attention to a few simple rules. First warm the pot (an earthenware one, preferably) by filling it with hot water; set it aside while the kettle boils. Measure a teaspoon of tea for each 8-ounce cup. If you wish, place the tea leaves in a perforated tea ball or infuser for easy removal.

Place tea and boiling water in the warm pot, and let the tea steep for 4½ to 5 minutes, then pour the tea (through a strainer if tea was placed loose in pot) at once. Some grandmotherly advice that holds up well: if you want stronger tea, use more *tea—longer brewing only makes the tea taste bitter.*

ORANGE-SPICED TEA

Here is a pleasantly flavored blend of tea with citrus and spices to keep on hand for a bit of variety at breakfast or brunch.

½ cup loose black tea leaves
1 stick (2 to 3 in.) cinnamon, broken into 3 or 4 pieces
¼ teaspoon *each* whole allspice and whole cloves
⅛ teaspoon ground ginger
2 pods whole cardamom, slightly crushed
2-inch strip lemon rind
2 teaspoons grated orange rind

1. Combine all ingredients in a covered jar, then let stand at room temperature for 2 to 3 days before using.

2. Brew as for unflavored tea, following procedure above.

Makes about ½ cup.

HOT CHOCOLATE

Morning chocolate may sound like kid stuff, but if you have ever tasted that offered as a breakfast beverage option in a good Swiss hotel, you know how satisfying it can be. Indeed, when chocolate arrived in Europe from the New World in the sixteenth century, drinking chocolate was as much a sensation as coffee would be a century later.

DOUBLE MOCHA

This luscious hot drink makes a brunch treat with brioches or other homemade bread and fresh fruit.

Tea balls and infusers help to produce a bracing cup of tea, allowing you to remove leaves as soon as the tea has steeped. Stainless steel lemon squeezer is German.

2½ tablespoons unsweetened cocoa
¼ cup sugar
    Dash salt
¼ cup hot water
2 cups milk
¼ teaspoon vanilla
2 cups hot espresso coffee
    Whipped cream (optional)

1. In a medium saucepan stir together cocoa, sugar, and salt. Blend in water. Bring to boiling over medium heat, stirring constantly for 1 minute.

2. Gradually add milk, stirring with a whisk. Heat until cocoa is steaming hot but just under the boiling point. Add vanilla, then beat with whisk until cocoa is frothy. Pour into 4 to 6 mugs, filling them half full.

3. Fill mugs with coffee. Top each with a dollop of whipped cream, if you wish.

Makes 4 to 6 servings.

ECSTATICALLY RICH HOT CHOCOLATE

Inspired by the legendary hot chocolate of the French Basque port city of Bayonne, this foamy cup is made with a combination of unsweetened and semisweet chocolate. Adding amaretto (see variation) transforms it into an Italian treat.

- **2 ounces (2 squares)** *each* **semisweet chocolate and unsweetened chocolate, coarsely chopped**
- **⅓ cup granulated sugar**
- **2 tablespoons brown sugar**
- **2 cups** *each* **milk and half-and-half (light cream)**
- **½ teaspoon vanilla**

1. In a 2-quart saucepan combine chocolate, sugars, milk, and half-and-half. Place over medium heat, stirring frequently with a whisk, until chocolate melts, sugar dissolves, and mixture is steaming hot but just under the boiling point. Reduce heat to keep chocolate hot.

2. Pour about half of the hot chocolate into a blender and whirl until frothy; stir into remaining hot chocolate in pan.

3. Mix in vanilla and serve at once.

Makes 4 to 6 servings.

Hot Chocolate Amaretto: Prepare preceding hot chocolate, omitting vanilla. Into each serving stir 1 tablespoon amaretto liqueur.

HOT CHOCOLATE, NEW MEXICO STYLE

Closer to its home in the Americas, hot chocolate is flavored with spices.

- **¼ cup** *each* **sugar and unsweetened cocoa**
- **½ teaspoon instant coffee powder or granules**
- **⅛ teaspoon salt**
- **1 cup water**
- **1 stick (2 to 3 in.) cinnamon**
- **2 cups milk**
- **1 cup half-and-half (light cream)**
- **1 tablespoon vanilla**
- **⅛ teaspoon ground cloves**

1. In a 2- to 3-quart saucepan mix sugar, cocoa, instant coffee, and salt. Stir in water; add cinnamon stick. Bring to boiling, reduce heat, and simmer for 5 minutes.

2. Add milk and half-and-half to cocoa mixture, stirring constantly; bring to boiling point, then remove from heat.

3. Mix in vanilla and cloves; remove cinnamon stick; beat until foamy, then serve.

Makes 1 quart (4 to 6 servings).

Frothy, cinnamon-spiced hot chocolate warms a breakfast of oranges and Mexican pan dulce or other sweet rolls.

FRUIT JUICES

Most people enjoy fruit in some form in the morning. When there isn't time to sit down to a half grapefruit or a bowl of cut fruit, a glass of orange or tomato juice is a quick and reasonably healthy substitute. Better still are freshly squeezed citrus juices, singly or in combination.

WINTER CITRUS WAKE-UP

Blending fruit juices results in some refreshing mixtures. Try this one: orange juice whirled with pink grapefruit and lime juice. The tart edge is bound to banish any morning grogginess.

- **4 oranges**
- **1 pink grapefruit**
- **1 lime**

1. Cut fruits in halves crosswise. Using a reamer or an electric juicer, squeeze juices from halved fruits.

2. Strain juices into blender or cocktail shaker. Whirl or shake until foamy and well blended. Cover and refrigerate if made ahead, then shake well before serving.

Makes 2 to 3 cups (3 to 4 servings).

PINK FRUIT JUICE FROTH

For a special occasion, pour this melon-pink fruit juice medley to drink through straws.

- **1 basket (about 2 cups) strawberries, hulled**
- **1 cup seeded, diced watermelon**
- **Juice of 2 oranges**
- **Juice of 1 lime**
- **1 to 2 tablespoons sugar**

1. In blender or food processor combine berries, melon, and orange and lime juices. Whirl or process until smooth and well blended.

2. Add sugar to taste. Cover and refrigerate if made ahead.

3. Serve each drink with a straw.

Makes about 3 cups (4 servings).

Four piquant fruits blend smoothly to make this appealing breakfast fruit juice drink. Whirl it together quickly in a blender or food processor for a morning treat.

A pan of this fragrant brew kept warm on an electric warmer or over a candle will perfume a winter brunch. It is delicious with homemade doughnuts or quick coffee cake.

- **2 tablespoons brown sugar**
- **1 teaspoon grated fresh ginger *or* ¼ teaspoon ground ginger**
- **¼ teaspoon whole allspice**
- **5 whole cloves**
- **3-inch strip lemon rind**
- **1 stick (2 to 3 in.) cinnamon**
- **1 quart cider *or* apple juice**

1. In a 2-quart saucepan combine brown sugar, ginger, allspice, cloves, lemon rind, and cinnamon stick.

2. Add cider and place over medium heat, stirring until sugar dissolves and mixture begins to boil. Cover, reduce heat, and simmer for 5 to 10 minutes to blend flavors.

3. Strain into heatproof mugs or cups.

Makes 4 to 6 servings.

HOT MULLED CRANBERRY PUNCH

It has the crimson color of mulled wine, and the spicy seasonings that flavor Swedish *glögg*—but this festive punch is a nonalcoholic fruit juice combination. Should you wish to spike it, add a tablespoon or two of brandy to each mug before straining in the punch.

- **2 cups water**
- **½ cup *each* sugar and raisins**
- **1 lemon, thinly sliced**
- **1 stick (2 to 3 in.) cinnamon**
- **1 teaspoon whole cloves**
- **2 whole pods cardamom, split**
- **1½ quarts (48 oz) cranberry juice cocktail**
- **1½ cups freshly squeezed tangerine or tangelo juice Whole blanched almonds**

1. In a 3- to 4-quart saucepan combine water, sugar, raisins, lemon, cinnamon stick, cloves, and cardamom. Bring to boiling, stirring until sugar is dissolved, then reduce heat and simmer, uncovered, for 5 minutes.

2. Add cranberry juice and tangerine juice. Heat, stirring occasionally, until mixture is steaming hot, but do not let it boil.

3. Place an almond in each heatproof mug or cup, and strain hot punch over it.

Makes 10 to 12 servings (about 10 cups).

Hot Spiced Cider is sure to be greeted warmly at a fall or winter brunch. It is shown here with squares of Banana-Nut Coffee Cake (the recipe is on page 86).

BREAKFAST-IN-A-GLASS

Fresh Fruit Blender Drink
Egg Bread Cinnamon Toast
Coffee

When time is short, you needn't let that stop you from enjoying a wholesome breakfast. Any of the blender drinks that follow can be whirled together in a jiffy, but are satisfying enough to keep you going all morning long.

Try each of the three flavors—then you will be able to use the same principle to put together your own breakfast creations. Hot cinnamon toast and a cup of coffee are nice additions to the basic breakfast, if time permits.

NECTARINE-PLUM DRINK

- **1 unpeeled nectarine, pitted and coarsely chopped**
- **1 unpeeled plum, pitted and coarsely chopped**
- **1 teaspoon lemon juice**
- **1 egg**
- **1 cup milk**
- **1 tablespoon Vanilla Sugar (see page 22)**
- **Pinch ground nutmeg**

1. Place all ingredients in blender. Whirl until smooth.

2. Serve at once, with a straw.

Makes 1 serving.

Whip up an appealing fruit shake for a full-meal breakfast drink. This is the strawberry version.

BANANA-LEMON DRINK

- **1 banana, peeled and cut in chunks**
- **1 egg**
- **1 tablespoon lemon juice**
- **½ teaspoon grated lemon rind**
- **½ cup *each* plain yogurt and milk**
- **1½ tablespoons Vanilla Sugar (see page 22)**
- **Pinch *each* ground cinnamon and nutmeg**

1. Place all ingredients in blender. Whirl until smooth.

2. Serve at once, with a straw.

Makes 1 serving.

FRESH STRAWBERRY DRINK

- **½ cup hulled, halved stawberries**
- **2 teaspoons lemon juice**
- **2 tablespoons Vanilla Sugar (see page 22)**
- **1 egg**
- **½ cup *each* plain yogurt and milk**

1. Place all ingredients in blender. Whirl until smooth.

2. Serve at once, with a straw.

Makes 1 serving.

CHAMPAGNE AND OTHER BRUNCH DRINKS

A sparkling wine makes a festivity of any breakfast or brunch. Still wines also complement many brunch menus: white or rosé wines are usually favored for their lightness.

You will wish to choose wines to enhance the specific dishes that make up your menu, of course. But brunch foods often lend themselves to the company of such fruity white wines as Chenin Blanc, Gewürztraminer, Gray Riesling, and Sauvignon Blanc. Have a look, also, at some of the blushing white wines made from red wine grapes — "white" Pinot Noir, Zinfandel, Cabernet, and so forth.

HAZEL'S RAMOS GIN FIZZ

Creamy drinks such as this gin fizz are always popular at brunch. This one is often served to precede Eggs Benedict, although both are so rich that you might prefer to team the fizzes with something a bit lighter.

- **1 cup cold half-and-half (light cream)**
- **½ cup gin**
- **¼ to ⅓ cup powdered sugar**
- **2 egg whites (¼ cup)**
- **½ teaspoon orange flower water**
- **1 cup crushed ice**
  Juice of 1 lemon (3 to 4 Tbsp)

1. In blender combine half-and-half, gin, powdered sugar, egg whites, and orange flower water. Add ice and lemon juice.

2. Blend at high speed until very foamy. Serve at once.

Makes 4 drinks.

Your blender makes quick work of such favorite brunch drinks as (from left) the Piña Colada, Tequila Sunrise, and Strawberry Daiquiri (recipe on page 19).

SPIRITED MILK PUNCH

Traditional for New Year's Day is this frothy milk punch made with brandy or whiskey.

- **1 cup brandy *or* whiskey**
- **2 cups cold milk**
- **¼ cup powdered sugar**
- **½ teaspoon vanilla**
- **½ cup crushed ice**
  Freshly grated nutmeg

1. In blender combine brandy, milk, powdered sugar, vanilla, and ice. Whirl until frothy and well combined.

2. Pour into wine glasses or punch cups. Grate a little nutmeg over each serving.

Makes 4 to 6 servings.

MIMOSA

Fresh orange juice and Champagne, accented by an orange liqueur such as Grand Marnier, combine to make the delicate brunch classic, the Mimosa.

- **1 cup freshly squeezed orange juice**
- **¼ cup orange-flavored liqueur**
- **1 bottle (750 ml) chilled brut *or* extra-dry Champagne**

1. Divide orange juice and orange liqueur evenly into each of 4 to 6 wine glasses.

2. Fill slowly with Champagne, mixing lightly to blend. Serve at once.

Makes 4 to 6 servings.

BELLINI

One of the loveliest of brunch drinks made with sparkling wine is the Bellini, made with the juice of fresh, white-fleshed peaches. A creation of Harry's Bar in Venice, it should be made with Prosecco, a sparkling wine from the Veneto region, to be authentic. However, Asti spumante is more widely exported and also produces an elegant drink.

- **2 medium-size white peaches (such as Babcock, Springtime, or Pat's Pride)**
- **1 tablespoon sugar**
- **1 teaspoon powdered ascorbic acid**
- **2 teaspoons lemon juice**
- **2 bottles (750 ml *each*) chilled Prosecco *or* Asti spumante**

1. Peel, pit, and coarsely chop peaches. Place in food processor or blender with

---

sugar, ascorbic acid, and lemon juice. Process or whirl until mixture is smooth.

2. Strain peach mixture into a small bowl; cover and refrigerate if made ahead.

3. Pour Asti spumante into 6- to 8-ounce wine glasses, filling them about half full. To each glass add about 1 tablespoon peach mixture and stir carefully to blend. Add more Asti spumante to almost fill glasses. Serve at once.

Makes about 12 drinks.

PIÑA COLADA

A favorite among the luscious creamy drinks made in the blender is this tropical-flavored combination of rum, coconut cream, and pineapple juice.

- **1 cup light rum**
- **¾ cup canned cream of coconut (sweetened)**
- **1½ cups pineapple juice**
- **½ cup half-and-half (light cream)**
- **1 cup crushed ice**
  Pineapple slices or spears, for garnish

1. In blender combine rum, coconut cream, pineapple juice, half-and-half, and ice.

2. Whirl at high speed until frothy and well combined.

3. Pour into 4 tall, footed or stemmed glasses. Garnish each with a pineapple slice or spear.

Makes 4 drinks.

TEQUILA SUNRISE

The tropical flavors of this handsome, tall drink make it a good choice to precede or accompany a brunch with a south-of-the-border or Hawaiian theme.

- **¼ cup grenadine syrup**
- **¾ cup tequila**
- **2 cups cold orange juice**
- **¼ cup orange-flavored liqueur**
- **2 cups crushed ice**
  Orange slices, for garnish

1. Divide grenadine equally into each of 4 tall, footed or stemmed glasses.

2. In blender combine tequila, orange juice, orange liqueur, and ice. Whirl at high speed briefly, just until all ingredients are well combined.

3. Pour tequila mixture slowly into glasses (to keep the grenadine layer intact). Garnish each drink with an orange slice. Serve at once with straws.

Makes 4 drinks.

SANGRIA

If your brunch has a Mexican accent—enchiladas or *Huevos Rancheros*, for example—a pitcher of fruity red wine is a fine companion.

> **Juice of 1 orange**
> **Juice of 2 lemons**
> **Juice of 1 lime**
> ⅓ **cup sugar**
> ¼ **cup orange-flavored liqueur**
> 1 **quart dry red wine**
> **Orange, lemon, lime, and strawberry slices**
> 1 **quart chilled club soda**

1. In a 2½- to 3-quart pitcher or a punch bowl, stir together fruit juices, sugar, and orange liqueur, mixing until sugar is dissolved. Mix in wine, then fruit slices to taste. Cover and refrigerate for 3 to 4 hours.

2. To serve, mix in club soda. Pour over ice in large wine glasses.

Makes 6 to 8 servings.

STRAWBERRY DAIQUIRI

You can make this pretty drink even when fresh strawberries are not in the market —it's done with frozen berries. The drink also has a spirited banana variation.

> 1 **egg white**
> **Granulated sugar**
> 1 **package (16 oz) frozen unsweetened strawberries, partially thawed**
> 1 **cup light rum**
> 2 **tablespoons lemon juice**
> 6 **tablespoons sugar**
> 1 **cup crushed ice**
> **Whole strawberries, for garnish (optional)**

1. To frost glasses, beat egg white in a small bowl until it begins to froth. Dip rims of glasses first in egg white, then in sugar. Set aside until frosted rims are set.

2. In blender combine strawberries, rum, lemon juice, the 6 tablespoons sugar, and ice. Whirl at high speed until frothy and well combined.

3. Pour into frosted glasses and serve at once, garnishing each drink with a strawberry if you wish. Serve with straws.

Makes 4 to 6 servings.

Banana Daiquiri: In place of strawberries use 2 medium bananas. Substitute ¼ cup lime juice for the lemon juice. Use 2 tablespoons sugar. Omit strawberry garnish.

BLOODY MARY

When you are serving a number of people, it is handy to have a blenderful of the seasoned tomato juice base in readiness to stir up this popular, tall vodka drink.

> 3 **cups cold tomato juice**
> ¼ **cup lemon juice**
> 1 **teaspoon *each* salt and Worcestershire sauce**
> ¼ **teaspoon *each* Tabasco sauce and prepared horseradish**
> **Pinch freshly ground pepper**
> ¾ **cup vodka**
> **Ice cubes (optional)**
> 4 **celery sticks**

1. In blender combine tomato juice, lemon juice, salt, Worcestershire sauce, Tabasco sauce, horseradish, and pepper. Whirl until well combined.

2. Pour vodka into 4 tall, slender glasses, using 3 tablespoons for each drink. Add ice cubes if you wish. Then divide tomato juice mixture among the glasses and stir well. Garnish each drink with a celery stick.

Makes 4 drinks.

Adding your own vigorous seasonings, instead of using a bottled mix, makes a Bloody Mary taste fresher and more authoritative.

Fruit at its simplest bestows elegance on day-to-day breakfasts. Look beyond bare bananas and berries to luscious fresh fruit combinations.

FLAVORFUL FRUITS

Fresh fruit makes breakfast seem more special. Even if it's just a matter of slicing a banana over your corn flakes or treating yourself to a small dish of perfect berries, the color and fragrance of fruit brightens the morning.

For a brunch, fruit can serve two purposes: a refreshing opener to the repast or an elegant dessert. Consider centering your buffet table with a glass bowl glowing with multicolored cut fruits—or concluding a more formal menu with the flourish of flambéed bananas.

Fruits are also rich repositories of a host of necessary nutrients. Apricots abound in a substance the body uses to make vitamin A (which helps fight colds and other infections and prevents night blindness). Citrus fruits—oranges, lemons, limes, grapefruit—contain vitamin C (ascorbic acid), as do strawberries. This vitamin promotes healing and may also have a role in preventing colds. Melons are a good source of vitamins A and C. The body can store vitamin A, but not vitamin C, so a food rich in the latter is needed every day for good health. All the better reason to form good breakfast habits.

A good habit, fortunately, need not become a dreary rut. The recipes in this chapter show how you can enjoy, on occasion, something special in the way of fruit. The choices are as wide as your greengrocer's seasonal stock allows. Make the most of them!

Jewel-toned fresh summer berries are the pick of the crop for breakfast. But every season has its luscious bounty of fruits for morning meals.

MELON BALLS SPUMANTE

Bubbly with a delicate Italian wine, this fruit medley can be served to open a brunch or as a light dessert with crisp cookies.

- **4 cups *each* 1-inch seeded Persian melon *or* cantaloupe and honeydew melon balls**
- **2 teaspoons lemon juice**
  Pinch freshly grated nutmeg
- **1 cup chilled Asti spumante**

1. In a glass serving bowl lightly mix melon, lemon juice, and nutmeg.

2. Slowly pour in Asti spumante; mix lightly. Serve at once, or cover and refrigerate for up to 2 hours.

3. Spoon melon into individual serving dishes, spooning liquid over.

Makes 6 to 8 servings.

Crisp Italian cookies from the bakery complement honeydew and Persian melon balls in Asti spumante for a sparkling brunch dessert.

PEACHES AND BLUEBERRIES WITH CREAM

Two summer favorites make a handsome combination to serve with cream, or to spoon over a puffy oven pancake (see page 69).

- **4 large peaches**
- **2 tablespoons lemon juice**
- **1 cup fresh *or* frozen (unsweetened) blueberries**
- **¼ cup sugar**
- **⅛ teaspoon ground nutmeg**
- **1 teaspoon grated lemon rind**
  Whipping cream or half-and-half (light cream)

1. To peel peaches, half-fill a large saucepan with hot water, bring to boiling, and add peaches, 2 at a time. Boil each batch for 30 seconds, then remove peaches and rinse with cold water. Use a small knife to slip off skins.

2. Slice peaches thinly (you should have about 5 cups); place in a medium bowl and mix lightly with lemon juice and blueberries. In a small bowl mix sugar, nutmeg, and lemon rind. Add sugar mixture to peach mixture, and mix lightly. Let stand for about 30 minutes before serving.

3. Spoon peach mixture into bowls. Pass a pitcher of cream to pour over peaches to taste.

Makes 6 servings.

FOUR SEASONS FRESH FRUIT BOWL

Starting with fruits you can find the year around—oranges, apples, and bananas—add fruits of the season to make a generous help-yourself fruit bowl at any time.

- **3 oranges**
- **2 unpeeled tart red apples, cored and diced**
- **2 firm-ripe bananas, sliced about ½ inch thick**
- **1 tablespoon lemon juice**
  Seasonal Fruits (suggestions follow)
  Vanilla Sugar, to taste (recipe follows)

1. Working over a large bowl, peel oranges close to fruit, cutting away the bitter white inner peel. Using a sharp paring knife, cut close to membranes, removing juicy segments of fruit and placing in bowl.

2. Add apples, bananas, and lemon juice; mix lightly. Gently mix in Seasonal Fruits. If made ahead, cover and refrigerate until ready to serve, up to 3 hours.

3. Sweeten with Vanilla Sugar if you wish. Makes 6 to 8 servings.

Seasonal Fruits: For *spring*, add 1 basket (about 2 cups) strawberries (hulled and cut in halves if large) and 2 kiwi fruit (peeled and sliced about ¼ inch thick). For *summer*, add 2 nectarines or peaches (peeled if you wish, pitted, and sliced) and ½ cup *each* seedless red or green grapes; blueberries, blackberries, or raspberries; pitted sweet cherries; and diced cantaloupe or honeydew melon. For *fall*, add 1 cup halved, seeded red grapes; 2 Bartlett pears (peeled, cored, and diced); and ¼ cup pomegranate seeds. For *winter*, add 1 winter pear (Anjou, Bosc, or Comice; peeled, cored, and diced); 1 cup peeled, cored, diced fresh pineapple; and 1 cup peeled, seeded, diced papaya. Substitute lime juice for lemon juice if you wish.

Vanilla Sugar: Embed half a vanilla bean in ½ cup granulated sugar in a covered jar for at least 24 hours. Replenish sugar as you use Vanilla Sugar to sweeten fruits.

ELEGANT ORANGES

Another way of beginning or ending a brunch is with slices of lightly spiced oranges drizzled with a liqueur such as Grand Marnier, Cointreau, or Triple Sec.

- **4 medium oranges**
- **1 tablespoon sugar, mixed with ¼ teaspoon cinnamon**
- **2 tablespoons orange-flavored liqueur**

1. Working over a wide, shallow bowl, peel oranges close to fruit, cutting away the bitter white inner peel. Thinly slice oranges crosswise, removing seeds if any. Spread orange slices in bowl.

2. Sprinkle evenly with sugar-and-cinnamon mixture, then with liqueur.

3. Let oranges stand, uncovered, at room temperature for ½ to 1 hour before serving in small bowls with juices spooned over.

Makes 4 to 6 servings.

BROILED PINK GRAPEFRUIT

A mixture of butter, brown sugar, and a touch of nutmeg gilds juicy pink grapefruit.

- **3 pink grapefruit**
- **¼ cup butter or margarine, softened**
- **¼ cup firmly packed light brown sugar**
- **⅛ teaspoon ground nutmeg**

1. Cut grapefruit in halves. Using a grapefruit knife, loosen fruit from skin around edges and between segments. Remove and discard seeds. Place grapefruit, cut sides up, in a shallow rimmed baking pan.

2. In a small bowl beat together butter, brown sugar, and nutmeg until smooth and well combined. Dot butter mixture evenly over the grapefruit halves.

3. Place beneath broiler, about 4 inches from heat. Broil until topping is melted, bubbling, and lightly browned (3 to 5 minutes). Serve hot.

Makes 6 servings.

Here is a fruit bowl for all seasons. The basic mix is made up of oranges, apples, and bananas—in winter, add a pear, pineapple, papaya, and lime juice (photo at left); in spring add strawberries and kiwi fruit.

HOT BUTTERED PLUMS

These fresh summer plums in a tart orange sauce are nice to serve from a chafing dish, either alone or as a topping for crêpes or crisp waffles.

    ¼ cup butter or margarine
    ½ cup sugar
    2 teaspoons cornstarch
    ⅛ teaspoon ground nutmeg
    4 cups quartered, pitted red
       plums
    ½ teaspoon vanilla
       Juice and grated rind of 1 small
       orange

1. In a large frying pan, melt butter over medium heat. Stir in sugar, cornstarch, and nutmeg. Mix in plums, turning to coat with sugar mixture. Cook, stirring occasionally, until juices form a thick sauce (3 to 5 minutes).

2. Remove from heat; gently stir in vanilla and orange juice and rind. Return to heat and stir until sauce boils and thickens slightly (2 to 3 minutes). Serve hot.

Makes 6 servings.

CINNAMON-PINK APPLESAUCE

Tiny red cinnamon candies give this homemade applesauce a spicy tang and hot pink color.

    6 medium-size (about 2 lbs) tart
       cooking apples, peeled, cored,
       and cut in chunks
    ¼ cup sugar
    2 tablespoons tiny red-hot
       cinnamon candies
    ¼ cup water

1. Place apples in a 2-quart saucepan with sugar, cinnamon candies, and water.

2. Bring to boiling, cover, reduce heat, and cook, stirring occasionally, until apples are very tender (15 to 20 minutes).

3. Stir with a fork until mixture has a saucelike consistency. (Put through a food mill or process until smooth in a food processor if you wish.)

4. Serve warm, at room temperature, or chilled.

Makes 6 servings.

SPICED RHUBARB

When pink stalks of rhubarb make their first appearance, it is a sign that winter is turning into spring—a happy message to convey at breakfast.

    4 cups diced rhubarb
    ½ cup sugar
    1 stick (2 to 3 in.) cinnamon
    3 whole cloves
    ⅛ teaspoon ground nutmeg
    ¼ cup cold water

1. In a heavy 2-quart saucepan combine all ingredients. Bring to boiling, cover, reduce heat, and simmer until mixture has a saucelike consistency (8 to 10 minutes).

2. Pour into a bowl, and let stand at room temperature until cool. Remove and discard cinnamon stick and cloves.

3. Serve at room temperature or chilled.

Makes 4 servings.

WINTER FRUIT COMPOTE

These dried fruits, plumped in spiced port, make a handsome combination. Enjoy them—cooked the night before—while a Sunday morning quiche bakes.

    ½ pound (about 1¼ cups) dried
       prunes
    1 package (6 oz) dried apricots
    1 stick (2 to 3 in.) cinnamon
    ½ lemon, thinly sliced
       Juice of 1 orange
    3 tablespoons brown sugar
       Water
    ¼ cup port wine

1. In a 2-quart saucepan combine prunes, apricots, cinnamon stick, lemon slices, and orange juice. Sprinkle with sugar. Add just enough water to barely cover fruits.

2. Bring to boiling, cover, reduce heat, and simmer until fruits are plump and tender (8 to 10 minutes).

3. Stir in port; transfer to a glass bowl. Serve fruits (with their liquid) warm, at room temperature, or chilled.

Makes 6 servings.

Summer offers the seasonal fruit bowl (left) such stunning choices as nectarines, peaches, seedless grapes, cherries, and berries. In fall give it a fresh face with red grapes, Bartlett pears, and a shower of crimson pomegranate seeds.

NUTTY BAKED APPLES

Rome Beauty or McIntosh apples are good for baking, and delicious stuffed with chopped nuts, brown sugar, and butter.

- **6 large baking apples**
- **⅓ cup finely chopped walnuts, pecans, *or* blanched almonds**
- **⅓ cup firmly packed brown sugar**
- **2 teaspoons butter or margarine, softened**
- **1 teaspoon grated lemon rind Water**

1. Core apples and remove about 1½ inches of peel around the stem end. Arrange in a buttered shallow baking dish just large enough to hold all the apples.

2. In a small bowl mix nuts, brown sugar, butter, and lemon rind. Divide mixture among cavities in apples. Add water to the dish to a depth of about ¼ inch.

3. Bake apples, uncovered, in a 375°F oven, basting occasionally with liquid from bottom of dish, until tender when pierced with a fork (40 to 45 minutes).

4. Serve hot or at room temperature.

Makes 6 servings.

ITALIAN BAKED APPLES WITH PRUNES

If you wish to serve these apples first thing in the morning, you can assemble the dish in its covered casserole the night before and refrigerate it. Then pop it into the oven as soon as you arise.

- **4 small tart cooking apples**
- **1 cup dried prunes**
- **½ teaspoon grated lemon rind**
- **1 teaspoon vanilla**
- **1 tablespoon lemon juice**
- **¼ cup water**
- **¼ teaspoon ground nutmeg**
- **⅓ cup sugar**

1. Core apples (do not peel) and place in a covered casserole just large enough to hold them. Around apples arrange prunes. Sprinkle with lemon rind, vanilla, lemon juice, and water. Mix nutmeg and sugar, and sprinkle evenly over fruits.

2. Cover and bake in a 350°F oven until apples and prunes are very tender (45 to 55 minutes).

3. Spoon an apple into each of 4 small soup or cereal bowls; break apples open with a spoon, and spoon prunes and juices over. Serve at once.

Makes 4 servings.

A homey Italian dessert — apples baked with prunes, lemon, and nutmeg — becomes a breakfast inspiration. It can be assembled the night before and baked in the morning.

CHUNKY SAUTEED APPLES WITH LEMON

For an out-of-the-ordinary family breakfast some winter weekend, bake gingerbread and serve it warm with this tart-sweet applesauce.

- **2 tablespoons butter**
- **5 medium-size tart cooking apples, peeled and cut in bite-size chunks**
- **1 teaspoon grated lemon rind**
- **1 tablespoon lemon juice**
- **⅛ teaspoon ground nutmeg**
- **½ cup sugar**
- **2 tablespoons pear brandy (optional)**

1. Heat butter in a large frying pan over moderately high heat until foamy. Mix in apples, lemon rind, lemon juice, and nutmeg. Cook, uncovered, stirring occasionally, until apples are almost tender (8 to 10 minutes).

2. Stir in sugar and cook, stirring gently, for about 2 minutes longer, until apples are tender to your taste. If you wish, mix in pear brandy and cook, stirring, until most of the liquid is reduced.

3. Serve warm, at room temperature, or chilled.

Makes 4 to 6 servings.

Tart fall apples, sautéed in butter with lemon and nutmeg, are served hot with freshly baked gingerbread and milk for a memorable family breakfast. For a brunch dessert, flavor the apples with a splash of pear brandy.

MAPLE APPLE CRISP

Bowls of this crumb-topped apple pudding can be served as you would hot cereal, to celebrate a fine fall day. If maple sugar is not available, use 1 cup of brown sugar.

- **½ cup *each* maple sugar and firmly packed light brown sugar**
- **½ cup all-purpose flour**
- **¼ teaspoon *each* ground cinnamon and nutmeg**
- **¼ cup firm butter or margarine**
- **6 medium-size tart cooking apples Whipping cream *or* half-and-half (light cream)**

1. Mix maple and brown sugars, flour, cinnamon, and nutmeg. Cut in butter until mixture is crumbly.

2. Peel, core, and slice apples (you should have about 5 cups); spread in a buttered 8- or 9-inch-square baking dish. Sprinkle sugar mixture evenly over apples, patting it together lightly.

3. Bake, uncovered, in a 350°F oven for 40 to 45 minutes, until topping is crisp and well browned and apples are tender.

4. Serve warm with cream.

Makes 6 servings.

BREAKFAST STRAWBERRY SHORTCAKE

Homemade biscuits, buttered while they are hot, distinguish this traditional shortcake from the Midwest. Although most would consider it a dessert, this shortcake is also irresistible for breakfast.

- **2 baskets (about 1 qt) strawberries**
- **½ cup sugar**
- **2 cups all-purpose flour**
- **1 tablespoon baking powder**
- **½ teaspoon salt**
- **½ cup firm butter or margarine**
- **1 egg**
- **⅓ cup half-and-half (light cream)**
  Half-and-half, for brushing
  Butter or margarine (optional)
  Whipped cream
  Vanilla Sugar (see page 22)

Treat yourself to a summer breakfast surprise—fresh strawberry short-cake with hot, buttery biscuits. It has most of the nutrients you need to start the day.

1. Hull strawberries, and cut about 2 cups of them in halves; place halved berries in a bowl, mix lightly with ¼ cup of the sugar, and let stand at room temperature for about 1 hour. Set whole berries aside.

2. In a mixing bowl stir together remaining ¼ cup sugar, flour, baking powder, and salt. Cut in ½ cup butter to form coarse crumbs.

3. Beat egg with the ⅓ cup half-and-half. Add egg mixture, all at once, to flour mixture; mix gently just until a soft dough forms. Turn dough out onto a floured board or pastry cloth, turning to coat lightly with flour. Knead lightly just until dough is smooth. Pat or roll out about ¾ inch thick. Cut into 2½- to 3-inch rounds. Place on an ungreased baking sheet. Brush tops lightly with half-and-half.

4. Bake biscuits in a 425°F oven until golden (12 to 15 minutes).

5. To serve shortcakes, split hot biscuits, and spread cut surfaces lightly with butter if desired. Place in shallow individual bowls and fill with sugared berries. Top with whipped cream and whole strawberries. Add Vanilla Sugar to taste.

Makes 6 to 8 servings.

BERRIES ROMANOFF

Here is an elegant conclusion for a stylish brunch—strawberries and raspberries cloaked in a silken sherried cream. The beaten egg yolk mixture that makes the sauce can be cooked several hours before serving and refrigerated.

- **3 egg yolks**
- **⅔ cup sugar**
- **⅔ cup dry Marsala or cream sherry**
- **3 cups strawberries**
- **1 cup raspberries**
- **⅔ cup whipping cream**

1. Combine egg yolks and sugar in top of a double boiler (off heat); beat until thick and pale. Mix in Marsala and place over simmering water. Cook, stirring constantly with a wire whisk, until thick (10 to 12 minutes).

2. Transfer egg yolk mixture to a large bowl, cover, and refrigerate until ready to serve.

3. Meanwhile, rinse berries carefully. Hull strawberries, reserving a few with leaves for garnish if you wish. Pat berries dry.

4. Whip cream until stiff; carefully fold into egg yolk mixture until blended. Fold in berries. Serve in glasses, garnishing with whole berries if you wish.

Makes 4 to 6 servings.

BANANAS FOSTER

A dramatic presentation characterizes this dish, which originated in New Orleans. Serve the flaming bananas over ice cream that has been scooped into individual dishes ahead of time and held in the freezer.

- **¼ cup butter or margarine**
- **⅓ cup firmly packed brown sugar**
- **4 firm-ripe bananas**
- **¼ teaspoon ground cinnamon**
- **⅓ cup banana liqueur**
- **½ cup rum**
  Rich vanilla ice cream

1. In a chafing dish over an alcohol flame or in a cook-and-serve frying pan, melt butter over medium heat. Stir in brown sugar; cook and stir until sugar melts and bubbles.

2. Peel bananas and cut them in halves lengthwise, then crosswise, making 4 pieces from each. Add to butter mixture; sprinkle evenly with cinnamon. Carefully turn bananas, spooning sugar mixture over them. Lightly mix in banana liqueur.

3. Warm rum very slightly in a small metal pan; add to banana mixture, ignite, stir for a few minutes, then spoon flaming bananas around ice cream in individual dishes.

Makes 4 servings.

BLACKBERRY COBBLER

When berries are in season, bake this luscious cobbler to serve for a summer breakfast on the back porch. It can be made in a large baking dish or in 4 individual ones.

> 3 to 4 cups fresh blackberries, boysenberries, or olallieberries
> ⅔ cup sugar
> 1 tablespoon lemon juice
> ¼ cup butter or margarine, softened
> ½ teaspoon vanilla
> ⅔ cup all-purpose flour
> 1 teaspoon baking powder
> ¼ teaspoon salt
> ⅛ teaspoon *each* ground cinnamon and nutmeg
> ½ cup milk
>   Whipping cream (optional)

Bubbling with blackberries, this cobbler has a cakelike topping and is a wonderful hot breakfast dish. Pour on cream to cool and enrich the berries.

1. Spread berries in a buttered shallow 2-quart baking dish; sprinkle evenly with ⅓ cup of the sugar and the lemon juice. (Or divide berries, sugar, and lemon juice among 4 buttered individual 2-cup baking dishes about 2 inches deep.)

2. Cream butter and remaining ⅓ cup sugar until fluffy. Beat in vanilla. Mix flour with baking powder, salt, cinnamon, and nutmeg. Add flour mixture to creamed mixture alternately with milk, beating until smooth after each addition. Spread over berries.

3. Bake in a 400°F oven for 35 to 40 minutes, until topping is well browned and springs back when center is touched lightly.

4. Serve warm or at room temperature, spooned into shallow bowls. Pour on cream if you wish.

Makes 4 to 6 servings.

Freshly Squeezed Orange Juice
Puffy Apple Fritters with Powdered Sugar and Cinnamon
Grilled Pork Sausages
Coffee *or* Milk

Choose your favorite tart apples for these crisply coated fritters. The batter contains beer, which makes it light and crisp when fried and adds a faintly malty flavor. The apple slices can be fried as long as an hour or two before serving, then reheated in the oven. Sift powdered sugar and a hint of cinnamon over them at the table.

PUFFY APPLE FRITTERS

> 1 cup all-purpose flour
> 1 cup beer
> 4 large apples, peeled and cored
>   All-purpose flour
>   Vegetable oil for deep frying
>   Powdered sugar
>   Ground cinnamon

1. In blender or food processor combine the 1 cup flour and beer. Whirl or process until smooth and well combined, stopping motor and scraping down sides of container with a rubber spatula once or twice to be sure all flour is incorporated. Pour batter into a shallow bowl.

2. Slice apples, crosswise, about ½ inch thick. Dust slices lightly with flour.

3. Pour oil to a depth of at least 2 inches into a large, deep, heavy pan. Heat oil to 375°F. Dip apple rings into batter, coating thoroughly. Fry, about 4 at a time, in heated oil for 2 to 3 minutes, turning once, until golden brown on both sides.

4. Remove apple fritters with a slotted spoon, drain quickly on paper towels, then sprinkle generously with powdered sugar and a pinch of cinnamon and serve hot.

Note: If made ahead, arrange fritters on several layers of fresh paper towels on baking sheets. Reheat in 350°F oven for 8 to 10 minutes.

Makes 4 to 6 servings.

Versatile eggs are a breakfast mainstay. Cook them in the shells, hard or soft. Fry or poach them. Or create a glorious omelet or soufflé.

EGGS
ANY STYLE

Can there be any single breakfast food more versatile than the egg? If time is short, you can cook it in and eat it from its own tidy little package. With only slightly more effort, you can crack the egg and sizzle it in butter or poach it in liquid.

To serve a crowd you can scramble a dozen at a time, and for showmanship, there are fluffy omelets and lofty soufflés.

Every one of these distinctly different dishes begins with an egg. An egg is delicious simply with salt, pepper, and perhaps a bit of butter or tastefully embellished with such natural companions as ham, bacon, cheese, seafood, or mushrooms.

Each style of egg cookery has its own requirements. One useful generalization is that eggs benefit from low-temperature cooking. Too much heat is likely to toughen an egg—the white is particularly sensitive—and make it rubbery.

A soft-cooked egg from an eggcup (photo at right) is a child's delight with cocoa, an orange, and Maple-Nut Bran Muffins (the recipe is on page 84).

Eggs offer infinite opportunities for breakfast variety. Cook them in the shell, fry or poach them, scramble them, or whip up an omelet or puffy soufflé.

EGGS COOKED IN THE SHELL

Whether soft- or hard-cooked, eggs will taste best if you adjust the heat so that the water in which they cook never quite boils. Ideally, you should see tiny bubbles form on the bottom of the pan and rise slowly to the surface without breaking it.

SOFT-COOKED EGGS

1. Fill a saucepan with just enough water to cover the number of eggs to be cooked. Bring to a simmer and carefully lower eggs into the water. Simmer, uncovered, for 3 to 5 minutes, until eggs are done to taste.

2. Serve each egg, in shell, in an eggcup, cracking top lightly with a spoon and peeling about ½ inch of shell so egg can be eaten from remainder of shell. Or quickly cut egg in half, then use a spoon to scoop egg out into a small, warm dish.

HARD-COOKED EGGS

1. Place eggs in a single layer in a saucepan and cover with cold water. Bring to boiling over high heat; then reduce heat so bubbles rise slowly to surface but do not break it. For tenderness and best color, the cooking water should *never boil* fully. Simmer, uncovered, for 20 minutes.

2. Pour off hot water, cover eggs with cold water, and let stand, changing cold water occasionally, until eggs are cool (about 30 minutes).

SHRIMP-CROWNED EGGS

A simple soft-cooked egg becomes quite another story when you top it with buttery little shrimp to stir into each spoonful. Another topping you might present in the same way is a teaspoon of caviar and a dollop of sour cream seasoned with chives.

    2 teaspoons butter or margarine
    1 green onion, finely chopped
  ¼ cup tiny peeled, cooked shrimp
    6 eggs
      Hot buttered toast strips

1. Melt butter in a small frying pan over medium heat. Mix in onion and stir just until limp. Add shrimp and mix lightly, just until shrimp are heated through. Remove from heat and keep warm.

2. Soft-cook eggs according to directions on page 29. Place eggs in eggcups and carefully slice off top fourth of each egg, using a serrated knife or egg scissors.

3. Scoop out and discard whites from egg tops. Fill each eggshell cap with about 2 teaspoons of the shrimp mixture. Quickly invert shrimp-filled tops onto the eggs and serve at once, accompanied by toast strips to dip into egg yolks.

Makes 6 servings.

EGG AND BROCCOLI CASSEROLE WITH HAM PINWHEEL BISCUITS

Fresh broccoli combines with sliced hard-cooked eggs to make a colorful brunch main dish. Accompany it with a salad of crisp romaine lettuce and orange sections.

- **1 bunch (1¼ to 1½ lbs) broccoli**
  Salted water
- **2 tablespoons butter or margarine**
- **1½ tablespoons all-purpose flour**
- **¼ teaspoon salt**
  Pinch *each* white pepper and ground nutmeg
- **1 cup milk**
- **¾ cup diced sharp Cheddar cheese (¼-in. cubes)**
- **4 hard-cooked eggs (see page 29), sliced**
  Ham Pinwheel Biscuits (recipe follows)

1. Cut off broccoli flowerets and separate into bite-size pieces. Trim and discard ends of stems; peel lower portion of stems. Slice stems crosswise about ¼ inch thick.

2. Cook flowerets and stems in a small amount of boiling salted water (or steam on a rack) until barely tender-crisp (4 to 6 minutes). Place in a colander; rinse well

Hard-cooked eggs in a nippy sauce with cheese and broccoli lie beneath ham-filled biscuits blanketing this appealing brunch casserole.

with cold water to cool broccoli. Drain well and set aside.

3. In a medium saucepan heat butter over moderate heat until bubbly. Blend in flour, salt, pepper, and nutmeg. Remove from heat and gradually blend in milk. Cook, stirring constantly, until thickened; remove sauce from heat. Lightly fold in broccoli, cheese, and eggs.

4. Spread broccoli mixture in a buttered 2-quart casserole. Place biscuits, cut sides down, around edge of casserole with one in center.

5. Bake casserole in a 425°F oven until biscuits are well browned and sauce is bubbly (25 to 30 minutes). Serve at once, lifting biscuits onto plates, then spooning broccoli mixture beside them.

Makes 4 to 6 servings.

Ham Pinwheel Biscuits: In a medium bowl mix 1½ cups all-purpose flour, 2 teaspoons baking powder, and ½ teaspoon salt. Cut in ⅓ cup firm butter or margarine until mixture is crumbly. Lightly mix in ⅔ cup milk to make a soft dough. Turn dough out on a lightly floured board or pastry cloth and knead gently just until dough holds together (about 30 seconds). Roll out to an 8- by 10-inch rectangle. Spread 1 tablespoon Dijon mustard evenly over dough, not quite to edges. Cover mustard-spread area with 4 thin slices boiled ham, overlapping them slightly if necessary.

Starting with an 8-inch edge, roll dough up jelly-roll fashion. Moisten edge and pinch to seal. Cut into 8 equal slices.

NIPPY EGG AND CHEESE BUNS

A hard-cooked egg alone, peeled and eaten out-of-hand, makes a minimal breakfast in a pinch. Better still, however, is an English muffin broiled with this combination of hard-cooked eggs, olives, and Cheddar cheese. To save time, you can make the filling ahead, then spread and broil the muffins in the morning.

- **2 cups shredded sharp Cheddar cheese**
- **1 can (4¼ oz) chopped ripe olives, well drained**
- **½ sweet red or green bell pepper, seeded and finely chopped**
- **4 green onions, thinly sliced**
- **2 hard-cooked eggs (see page 29), chopped**
- **2 tablespoons catsup**
- **2 teaspoons prepared mustard**
- **4 whole wheat English muffins, split**

1. Mix cheese, olives, red or green pepper, onions, eggs, catsup, and mustard until well combined.

2. Arrange English muffins on a baking sheet and broil until cut sides are slightly browned. Remove from oven and divide egg mixture evenly among the 8 muffin halves, spreading it to edges.

3. Broil, about 4 inches from heat, until cheese is melted and lightly browned (3 to 5 minutes).

Makes 4 servings (2 muffin halves each).

FRIED EGGS

Two styles of frying turn out an equally acceptable egg — you can baste it with the butter in which it cooks until the yolk is done to your taste, or cover it so that steam does the job. If you use a frying pan with a nonstick surface, you can use less butter — or none at all.

BASIC FRIED EGGS

1. Using a frying pan just large enough to hold the number of eggs to be cooked, add about ½ tablespoon butter or margarine for each egg. Place pan over medium heat, swirling until butter melts and begins to sizzle.

2. Carefully break eggs into pan. Reduce heat to medium-low and cook, uncovered, occasionally spooning butter over eggs, until whites are set and a pale, translucent film covers yolks. *Or*, after adding eggs to pan and reducing heat, cover, and cook until eggs are done to your liking as in first method.

CHEESE-SPECKLED EGGS

For a change of pace, sprinkle fried eggs with cheese and bacon bits shortly before they finish cooking.

- **2 tablespoons butter or margarine**
- **4 eggs**
- **¼ cup shredded sharp Cheddar *or* provolone cheese**
- **1 tablespoon *each* packaged bacon bits and finely chopped fresh parsley**

1. Melt butter in a medium frying pan over moderate heat, swirling until butter melts and begins to sizzle. Carefully break eggs into pan. Reduce heat to medium-low, cover, and cook for 1 minute.

2. Sprinkle evenly with cheese and bacon, cover again, and continue cooking until eggs are cooked to your liking (1½ to 2 minutes).

3. Serve sprinkled with parsley.

Makes 2 or 4 servings.

FRIED EGGS WITH TOMATO SAUCE, MEXICANA

Served on hot tortillas and blanketed with a chile-spiked tomato sauce, these spirited eggs are known in Mexico as *huevos rancheros*. The sauce can be made ahead, then reheated, to simplify last-minute preparation. Accompany the eggs with refried beans and a basket of additional hot, buttered tortillas.

- **1 medium onion, chopped**
- **1 tablespoon *each* butter or margarine and olive oil**
- **1 clove garlic, minced or pressed**
- **1 small dried hot red chile, crushed *or* 1 canned green chile, seeded and chopped**
- **1 can (1 lb) tomatoes**
- **1 teaspoon chili powder**
- **½ teaspoon salt**
- **¼ teaspoon sugar**
- **8 corn tortillas**
  Oil for frying
- **8 eggs**
- **¼ cup shredded Monterey jack *or* mild Cheddar cheese**
  Sprigs of cilantro (Chinese parsley), for garnish
  Sliced avocado
  Refried Beans (recipe follows)

1. In a medium frying pan cook onion in mixture of butter and olive oil over moderate heat until soft but not browned. Mix in garlic, red or green chile, tomatoes and their liquid (break up tomatoes with a fork), chili powder, salt, and sugar. Bring to boiling, cover, reduce heat, and simmer for 30 minutes. Uncover and cook for about 5 minutes longer, until sauce is reduced to about 1¾ cups. Keep warm; or make ahead, refrigerate, and then reheat.

2. Fry tortillas in about ½ inch of hot oil in a large frying pan until limp, or if you prefer, until crisp and lightly browned. Drain on paper towels and keep warm in a 250°F oven.

3. Pour out most of the oil, then fry eggs (see page 30) in the same pan until done to your liking.

4. For each serving, arrange 2 prepared tortillas on a large warm plate. Top each with an egg, then spoon on hot tomato sauce and sprinkle with cheese. Garnish with cilantro sprigs and avocado. Accompany with hot Refried Beans.

Makes 4 servings (2 eggs each).

Refried Beans: In a medium frying pan, cook 1 small onion (finely chopped) in 1 tablespoon *each* butter or margarine and olive oil, stirring until tender and lightly browned. Mix in 1 small clove garlic (minced or pressed), 1 small can (8¼ oz) refried beans, and ¼ teaspoon chili powder. Cook over medium heat, stirring occasionally, until beans are heated through (3 to 5 minutes). Mix in ⅓ cup shredded Monterey jack or mild Cheddar cheese until melted. Makes 4 servings.

The breakfast of Mexican ranches —fried eggs on tortillas in a fiery tomato sauce, with cheese, avocado, and refried beans—is a weekend treat for brunch.

FRIED EGG MUFFIN SANDWICHES

One might describe this dish, borrowed from a popular fast-food concept, as no-fuss Eggs Benedict. You just pick it up in both hands and eat it as a sandwich.

Try different combinations of types of ham and cheese for variety: baked ham with Cheddar cheese; boiled ham with Swiss cheese; coppa or prosciutto with provolone or Fontina cheese; Black Forest ham with Muenster cheese.

- **2 English muffins, split**
- **3 tablespoons butter or margarine**
- **2 eggs**
- **2 thin slices ham, cut to fit muffins approximately**
- **2 thin slices cheese**

1. Toast muffins and keep them warm.

2. To a large frying pan add butter and swirl over medium heat until butter melts and begins to sizzle. Carefully break eggs into pan. (Use egg poaching rings—see below—if you wish, to be sure egg has same shape as muffin; remove them after whites are set.) Add ham slices beside eggs. Reduce heat to medium-low, and cook, uncovered, occasionally spooning butter over eggs, until whites are set and a pale, translucent film covers yolks. Turn ham slices once.

3. Place a cheese slice carefully on top of each egg.

4. To assemble each sandwich, place a ham slice on bottom half of muffin, top with egg and cheese, then cover with top half of muffin. Serve hot.

Makes 2 servings.

POACHED EGGS

Elaborate poached egg dishes become much easier to manage when you learn a simple trick: the eggs can be poached hours ahead, even the night before, and refrigerated in a bowl of ice water. Shortly before you are ready to serve the eggs, warm them in a bowl of hot water.

BASIC POACHED EGGS

1. Immerse eggs (in shells) in rapidly boiling water for 5 seconds; remove eggs and set them aside. Pour water into a large, deep pan to a depth of about 2½ inches; place over high heat until water begins to boil. Then adjust heat so that water barely bubbles. Break eggs directly into water and cook gently until whites are firm (about 3 minutes).

2. Remove poached eggs from cooking water with a slotted spoon and serve at once, or immerse them in a bowl of ice water. Cover and refrigerate for several hours or overnight.

3. To reheat eggs, transfer to a bowl of water that is just hot to the touch and let stand 5 to 10 minutes.

POACHED EGGS WITH SORREL

Sorrel, a delightfully tart green, makes a flavorsome bed for poached eggs served with a creamy cheese sauce. If sorrel is not available, fresh spinach may be substituted, although it won't contribute quite such a distinctive taste.

- **8 eggs**
  Sherried Swiss Cheese Sauce (recipe follows)
- **1 shallot, finely chopped or 2 tablespoons finely chopped mild onion**
- **3 tablespoons butter or margarine**
- **6 cups lightly packed fresh sorrel or spinach leaves (stems removed), slivered**
  Pinch each salt, white pepper, and ground nutmeg
  Paprika and snipped chives, for garnish

1. Poach eggs according to directions at left.

2. Prepare cheese sauce; keep warm (or reheat if made ahead and refrigerated), covered, in a double boiler over simmering water.

3. Reheat eggs if poached ahead (see step 3, at left).

4. In a large frying pan cook shallot in butter over medium heat until soft and lightly browned. Stir in sorrel and cook just until it is wilted. Season with salt, pepper, and nutmeg. Divide mixture evenly into 4 warm, shallow individual casseroles.

5. Top each serving with 2 warm poached eggs. Spoon hot cheese sauce over eggs. Garnish with paprika and chives.

Makes 4 servings.

Sherried Swiss Cheese Sauce: Melt 2 tablespoons butter or margarine in a 1½-quart saucepan. Stir in 1½ tablespoons all-purpose flour and a pinch *each* white pepper, nutmeg, and cayenne; cook until bubbly. Remove from heat and gradually mix in 1 cup half-and-half (light cream). Return to heat and cook, stirring, until thickened and bubbly. Stir in 1 cup shredded Swiss cheese until melted, then mix in ¼ cup dry sherry. Cover and refrigerate if made ahead. Makes about 1⅔ cups.

HELP FOR POACHING EGGS

Perfectly shaped poached eggs—cooked in the classic manner, in simmering water—can be difficult to achieve, especially if you are trying them for the first time. But help is available if you seek it out.

From England come deep, round rings. Or from France, egg-shaped perforated stands. Either gives a poached egg a regular shape and largely prevents the white from drifting away from the yolk as the egg cooks.

To use either shape, first butter it well or spray it with a vegetable oil nonstick coating. Place it in the pan with the simmering water, break the egg into the form, then cook as directed on this page.

The rings can also be used for frying eggs—handy if you want them exactly round to match an English muffin.

In the absence of either of these forms, you might also use rings from wide-mouth canning jars (although, because they are grooved, eggs are more likely to stick to them).

EGGS BENEDICT BRUNCH FOR EIGHT

Hazel's Ramos Gin Fizz
(see page 18)
Eggs Benedict
**Steamed Broccoli or
Asparagus Spears**
Bite-Size Fruits
Chocolate-Almond Cookie Bark
White Wine   Coffee

Creamy Ramos Fizzes (for 8 people, make 2 batches) should please your guests while you assemble the elegant egg dish. It is really not difficult to manage when you have poached the eggs in advance—several hours or a day ahead.

Depending on the season, broccoli or asparagus can share the delicious Hollandaise sauce with the eggs. The sauce can also be made well before your brunch. If you reheat it, be sure to keep the temperature of the water in the lower part of the double boiler below the boiling point. Too much heat can spoil the sauce.

With the eggs, serve coffee or a full-bodied white wine such as a dry Fumé Blanc.

After such a rich repast, keep dessert light. Select fruits that can be eaten with fingers or speared with wooden picks: in spring and summer try seedless grapes, whole strawberries, stemmed sweet cherries, and melon balls; for fall or winter, chunks of fresh pineapple and papaya, thick-sliced bananas (drizzled with lime or lemon juice to prevent discoloring), and thin wedges of ripe pears and tart apples. The irregular pieces of buttery-sweet cookie "bark" are a welcome accompaniment.

EGGS BENEDICT

16 eggs
   Hollandaise Sauce (recipe follows)
1 pound Canadian bacon or English muffin-size ham, cut in 16 slices
4 to 6 tablespoons butter or margarine
8 English muffins, split

1. Poach eggs according to directions on page 32, and refrigerate until ready to reheat.

2. Prepare sauce and keep it warm over hot (*not* boiling) water in a double boiler.

3. In a large frying pan over moderate heat cook Canadian bacon or ham in a little of the butter, adding more butter as needed (1 tablespoon at a time), until meat is lightly browned on both sides. Keep warm.

4. Reheat poached eggs as directed on page 32.

5. Broil split English muffins until crisp and golden brown.

6. For each serving, place 2 muffin halves on a warm plate and cover each with (in order) Canadian bacon, poached egg, and Hollandaise sauce. Serve at once.

Makes 8 servings.

Hollandaise Sauce: In a small pan melt 1 cup (½ lb) butter or margarine over medium heat until hot and foamy. While butter is melting, in blender or food processor place 3 eggs, 3 tablespoons lemon juice, 1 teaspoon Dijon mustard, and a pinch cayenne pepper. Turn blender or food processor on and begin pouring in hot butter in

Start with Eggs Benedict and fresh asparagus, both with Hollandaise Sauce. Then follow with fresh fruits and buttery-crisp chocolate chip cookies to eat with your fingers.

a slow, steady stream; whirl or process until all butter is added and sauce is smooth, frothy, and slightly thickened. Serve warm. Makes about 2 cups.

CHOCOLATE-ALMOND COOKIE BARK

¾ cup butter or margarine, softened
⅓ cup *each* granulated sugar and firmly packed light brown sugar
2 tablespoons coffee-flavored liqueur
1½ cups all-purpose flour
1 package (6 oz) semisweet chocolate pieces
½ cup slivered almonds

1. In large mixer bowl cream butter and sugars, beating until light and fluffy. Gradually blend in coffee liqueur.

2. Gradually add flour, mixing until blended. Stir in chocolate pieces.

3. Spread mixture evenly in an ungreased shallow 15- by 10-inch baking pan. Sprinkle evenly with almonds, pressing them lightly into dough.

4. Bake in a 375°F oven until cookies are well browned (18 to 20 minutes). Cool completely in pan on a wire rack, then turn out and break into irregular pieces.

Makes about 4 dozen cookies (about 1½ lbs).

POACHED EGGS WITH CHICKEN LIVERS

Raspberry wine vinegar, a favored seasoning of *nouvelle cuisine* enthusiasts, enhances the flavor of buttery chicken livers — a delicious foil for poached eggs on toast. Accompany this brunch dish with creamed spinach or asparagus spears.

- 6 eggs
- 6 tablespoons butter or margarine
- 6 slices firm white bread, crusts trimmed
- 1 pound chicken livers, cut in halves
- 2 shallots, finely chopped *or* ¼ cup finely chopped mild onion
- ½ teaspoon salt
  Freshly ground white *or* black pepper
- 2 tablespoons raspberry wine vinegar *or* tarragon white wine vinegar
  Chopped fresh parsley, for garnish

1. Poach eggs according to directions on page 32, and refrigerate until ready to reheat.

2. Melt 3 tablespoons of the butter in a large frying pan over medium-low heat, add bread, and cook, turning once, until slices are crusty and well browned on both sides. Remove to warm plates and keep warm.

3. Reheat poached eggs as directed on page 32.

4. To pan in which bread was browned add remaining 3 tablespoons butter, and increase heat to medium-high. Add chicken livers and shallots and cook livers, turning carefully, until well browned on all sides. As livers brown, remove them from pan. (They should remain moist and pink in centers.) Sprinkle with salt and add pepper to taste. When all livers are removed from pan, add vinegar to pan and cook, stirring, to dissolve pan drippings. Remove from heat, return livers to pan, and stir lightly to coat with drippings. Keep liver mixture warm.

5. Place a warm egg on each toast slice. Spoon chicken livers and their liquid around eggs. Sprinkle with parsley. Serve at once.

Makes 6 servings.

POACHED EGGS IN BAKED POTATOES

Based on an old French recipe for a country supper dish, these poached eggs also make a splendid brunch. Serve them with broccoli spears and follow with a dessert of fruit compote and ginger cookies. The egg-filled potatoes can be assembled in advance, then baked.

- 4 large baking potatoes
- ¼ cup butter or margarine
- 4 eggs
- 2 to 3 tablespoons milk
- ¼ teaspoon salt
  Pinch *each* white pepper and ground nutmeg
- 1 cup (about ¼ lb) julienne ham strips
  Mornay Sauce (recipe follows)
- ¼ cup *each* soft bread crumbs and shredded Parmesan cheese

1. Scrub potatoes and pat dry; rub skins lightly with a little of the butter and pierce each in several places with a fork. Bake in a 450°F oven for 50 minutes to 1 hour, until tender when pierced.

2. Poach eggs according to directions on page 32; refrigerate until ready to use.

3. When potatoes are cool enough to handle, cut a slice about ½ inch thick from the top of each, reserving slices. Carefully scoop out most of the inside of each potato; measure 1½ cups potato (reserve any remaining potato for other uses) into a mixing bowl. Add 1 tablespoon of the remaining butter, 2 tablespoons of the milk, salt, pepper, and nutmeg. Beat until fluffy, adding up to 1 tablespoon more milk to make a smooth (but not too soupy) mixture.

4. Return mashed potatoes to potato shells, and use the back of a spoon to make an egg-shaped hollow in each.

5. Cook ham in 1 tablespoon more of the butter in a medium frying pan, stirring until crisp and lightly browned.

6. Into the hollow in each potato place 1 tablespoon of the sauce, a fourth of the ham, and a drained poached egg. Place potatoes on a baking sheet or in shallow individual casseroles and spoon remaining sauce evenly over eggs. Top each potato with a tablespoon *each* of bread crumbs and Parmesan cheese. Melt remaining butter and drizzle evenly over tops of potatoes. Place slices cut from tops beside potatoes.

7. Bake in a 450°F oven for 10 to 15 minutes, until potatoes are heated through and topping browns lightly. Serve at once, with a top slice perched beside each potato.

Makes 4 servings.

Mornay Sauce: In a small saucepan melt 1 tablespoon butter or margarine over medium heat. Stir in 1 tablespoon flour, ⅛ teaspoon salt, and a pinch *each* white pepper and nutmeg; cook until bubbling. Remove from heat and gradually mix in 1 cup half-and-half (light cream); cook, stirring, until thick. In a small bowl beat 1 egg yolk; stir in a little of the hot sauce, then return mixture to pan. Cook over low heat, stirring constantly, until thick. Mix in ⅓ cup shredded Swiss cheese until melted, then remove from heat.

POACHED EGGS WITH LEEKS

A touch of caviar adds an elegant finish to poached eggs served on sautéed sliced leeks with a peppery cream sauce. For a superb brunch, add white wine and warm croissants or toasted English muffins.

- 8 eggs
- 3 large leeks
- 2 tablespoons butter or margarine
- ⅓ cup dry white wine
- ⅔ cup whipping cream
- 1 teaspoon *each* lemon juice and Dijon mustard
- ¼ teaspoon *each* salt and white pepper
- 1 tablespoon finely chopped fresh parsley
- 2 tablespoons black *or* red (or 1 tablespoon *each*) caviar

1. Poach eggs according to directions on page 32, and refrigerate until ready to reheat.

2. Cut off root ends of leeks; remove coarse outer leaves. Cut off upper parts of green tops, leaving about 10-inch-long leeks. Split lengthwise, from stem ends, cutting to within about 1 inch of root ends. Soak in cold water for several minutes; then separate leaves under running water to rinse away any clinging grit; drain well. Slice about ⅛ inch thick.

3. In a large frying pan melt butter over medium heat. Add sliced leeks; cook, stirring often, until leeks are tender and bright green (6 to 8 minutes). Remove leeks and divide them into 4 individual shallow au gratin dishes; keep warm.

4. Reheat poached eggs as directed on page 32.

5. To pan in which leeks were cooked add wine, whipping cream, lemon juice, mustard, and salt and pepper. Bring mixture to boiling and cook, stirring, until thickened and reduced to about ½ cup. Remove from heat and mix in parsley.

6. Place 2 warm eggs on top of leeks in each dish; spoon cream sauce over and around them, dividing it evenly; then top each egg with a dollop of caviar. Serve at once.

Makes 4 servings.

SCRAMBLED EGGS

When the cupboard is otherwise bare, you can always count on scrambled eggs for an enjoyable, quick, and nourishing breakfast or brunch. It's easy to add other ingredients to make the eggs more interesting, and even the least skilled beginner can learn the fundamentals of scrambling creamy, golden eggs.

Place the eggs in a bowl large enough to allow for brisk beating. Season with salt —about ¼ teaspoon for each 3 eggs (unless you plan to add other salty ingredients) — and a pinch of pepper. Add about 1 tablespoon of water, milk, or cream for each 3 eggs. Then beat with a fork, wire whisk, or egg beater until yolks and whites are completely blended

As with other types of eggs, cooking scrambled eggs over moderate to low heat assures that they will be moist and tender. Heat butter or margarine in a frying pan, then add the egg mixture. As the eggs begin to set, slowly stir the mixture with a wooden spoon or spatula, lifting cooked portions and letting the uncooked eggs flow underneath. Cook just until eggs are set, but still shiny and moist looking.

Other ingredients might be added to the butter in the same pan in which the eggs are to be scrambled. For example, cook onions, chopped green pepper, sliced mushrooms, or bits of ham first, then reduce heat before adding the eggs. Or, sprinkle the eggs with your favorite shredded cheese when they are nearly cooked. A scattering of snipped fresh parsley or other herbs at the finish also adds flavor.

CALICO SCRAMBLED EGGS

Colorful red pepper and green onions dot these scrambled eggs.

- ½ **cup finely chopped sweet red bell pepper**
- 6 **green onions, thinly sliced**
- ¼ **cup butter or margarine**
- 8 **eggs**
- 2 **tablespoons water or milk**
- ½ **teaspoon salt**
  Pinch white pepper

1. Cook red pepper and green onions in butter in a large frying pan over medium heat, stirring occasionally, until vegetables are soft but not browned.

2. In a bowl, beat eggs with water, salt, and pepper until well combined. Add egg mixture, all at once, to vegetable mixture. Reduce heat to low and cook, stirring lightly as eggs begin to thicken, until eggs are creamy and softly set. Serve at once.

Makes 4 servings.

Hot coffee, chilled tomato juice, and chive and ham-sprinkled Scrambled Eggs in a Crispy Crust make a colorful and complete breakfast.

SCRAMBLED EGGS IN A CRISPY CRUST

Serve fluffy scrambled eggs in a baked pastry for an unusual presentation. You can bake the crust ahead, then reheat it in the oven while preparing the eggs.

  Crisp Wheat Pastry (recipe follows)
- 8 **eggs**
- 2 **tablespoons water**
- ½ **teaspoon salt**
  Pinch *each* ground nutmeg and white pepper
- ¼ **pound thinly sliced Westphalian ham *or* prosciutto, julienne cut**
- 6 **tablespoons butter or margarine**
  Snipped chives *or* chopped fresh parsley, for garnish

1. Prepare pastry as directed, bake, and keep warm; if baked ahead, reheat in a 350°F oven until heated through (6 to 8 minutes).

2. In a large bowl beat eggs with water, salt, nutmeg, and pepper until well combined.

3. In a small frying pan cook ham strips in 2 tablespoons of the butter until lightly browned; keep warm.

4. Melt 3 tablespoons of the remaining butter in a large frying pan over low heat. Add egg mixture all at once. Cook, stirring lightly as eggs begin to thicken, until eggs are creamy. Cut remaining 1 tablespoon butter into bits, and add to eggs, stirring until softly set.

5. Spoon scrambled eggs into hot pastry. Scatter ham strips evenly over eggs, sprinkle lightly with chives or parsley, and serve at once.

Makes 4 to 6 servings.

Crisp Wheat Pastry: Mix ¾ cup unbleached all-purpose flour, ⅓ cup graham or whole wheat flour, ½ teaspoon salt, and ¼ teaspoon sugar. Cut in ¼ cup firm butter or margarine, 2 tablespoons lard, and 2 tablespoons grated Parmesan cheese until crumbly. Gradually mix in 1 teaspoon lemon juice and 1 to 1½ tablespoons cold water until mixture clings together.

Press dough into a flattened ball. Roll out on a floured board or pastry cloth to fit a 9-inch pie pan. Fit into pie pan; trim and flute edge. Pierce all over with a fork to prevent pastry from bubbling. Bake in a 450°F oven until lightly browned (10 to 12 minutes).

ITALIAN EGG AND VEGETABLE SCRAMBLE

Potatoes, Italian sausage, onion, green pepper, and tomato make this a hearty, late-morning brunch dish with toasted Italian or French bread and strong coffee or a fruity red wine.

- 2 tablespoons butter or margarine
- 1 tablespoon olive oil
- 1 medium potato, cut in ½-inch cubes
- ½ pound Italian sausages
- 1 small onion, thinly sliced and separated into rings
- ¼ cup finely chopped green pepper
- 8 eggs
- 2 tablespoons half-and-half (light cream)
- ½ teaspoon salt
- ⅛ teaspoon dried oregano
- 1 firm-ripe tomato, seeded and chopped
  Buttered, toasted Italian or French bread
- ¼ cup shredded Parmesan cheese
  Chopped fresh parsley, for garnish

1. Heat butter and oil in a large frying pan. Add potato and begin cooking over medium heat, stirring occasionally. Meanwhile, remove sausage casings and crumble the meat. Add to frying pan, cooking and stirring until lightly browned. Add onion and green pepper, cooking and stirring occasionally until onions are limp and potatoes are done.

2. In a bowl, beat eggs with half-and-half, salt, and oregano until well combined. Add tomatoes and egg mixture, all at once, to vegetable mixture. Reduce heat to low and cook, stirring lightly as eggs begin to thicken, until eggs are creamy and softly set.

3. Spoon eggs over slices of hot buttered toast, and sprinkle with cheese, then parsley.

Makes 4 to 6 servings.

A quick, French-style, folded omelet is the heart of many a breakfast or brunch. Almost anything is delicious inside—fresh vegetables, fruits, cheese, seafood, or ham or other meats.

OMELETS AND FRITTATAS

If scrambled eggs enjoy an anyone-can-do-it reputation, the omelet, by contrast, is often thought by novice cooks to be somewhat intimidating. Perhaps it does require a bit of practice to turn an omelet out smoothly. But once the knack is learned, making an omelet can be the quickest and most delicious route to a great breakfast or brunch.

One of the nicest things about omelets is that they can be filled with virtually anything you have in the refrigerator—cheese, sautéed vegetables, or bits of meat or seafood. Mastering the art of making fine omelets can earn you the reputation of being a great cook. And all it takes is eggs and a few odds and ends (even leftovers), artfully combined.

Although you might make a single 4- to 6-egg omelet and divide it in half to serve two, for three or more people the most practical route is to cook individual omelets. Prepare fillings, keeping them warm if necessary. Beat eggs with seasonings in a large bowl. Have butter at hand.

Then, using one or more omelet pans, cook and fill an omelet for each person. Omelet-making is so quick that one cook can serve several people in just a few minutes. If you are entertaining guests who enjoy cooking—and kitchen space permits—why not let each person turn out his or her own omelet!

BASIC OMELETS

- 9 eggs
- 3 tablespoons water
- ½ teaspoon salt
  Pinch *each* ground nutmeg and white pepper
- 3 to 4 tablespoons butter or margarine

1. In a large bowl beat eggs with water, salt, nutmeg, and pepper until well blended (about 30 seconds).

2. For each omelet heat about 1 tablespoon of the butter in an 8-inch omelet pan over medium-high heat until it begins to foam. Pour in a third to a fourth of the egg mixture.

3. At first, slide pan back and forth to keep omelet from sticking. As the bottom begins to set, slip a thin spatula under eggs, tilting pan and lifting cooked portion to let uncooked egg mixture flow under it to the center. Repeat until most of the omelet is set, but center and top are still moist and creamy.

4. For a filled omelet, spoon filling across center in line with handle. Have a warm serving plate ready. Loosen one side of the omelet with spatula and fold it about a third over the remainder. Then hold pan over serving plate so the other side begins to slide out. Flip omelet so previously folded side folds over, producing an omelet folded into thirds with center third on top.

Makes 3 or 4 individual omelets.

OMELET TIPS

The drawings below will help you to master the technique of turning out a fine omelet every time.

As egg mixture sets, tilt pan and gently lift cooked portions with a spatula, enabling the uncooked eggs to flow underneath.

When most of the omelet is set but top is still slightly moist, spoon filling across center in a line with the handle.

With warm serving plate in readiness, make first fold by loosening omelet and folding a third of it (from far side) toward the middle.

Tip pan with unfolded edge of omelet over plate, guiding with spatula, then flip quickly so previously folded edge turns over.

An omelet (this one has tiny shrimp and diced avocado) makes a perfect, lazy-morning breakfast.

SHRIMP AND AVOCADO OMELET

The filling for this omelet requires virtually no cooking—just warming through. The combination is delicious with sprouted wheat bread toast.

- 6 **green onions, thinly sliced**
- 6 **tablespoons butter or margarine**
- ¼ **pound small peeled, cooked shrimp**
- 1 **teaspoon lemon juice**
  Basic Omelets (see page 37)
- 1 **medium avocado, peeled, seeded, and diced**
- 3 **to 4 tablespoons sour cream**

1. In a medium frying pan over moderate heat cook onions in 2 tablespoons of the butter until limp and bright green. Add shrimp and lemon juice, stirring just until shrimp are heated through. Keep warm.

2. Immediately prepare 3 or 4 Basic Omelets, following directions on page 37, and cooking them in remaining butter. Use a third or a fourth of the shrimp filling for each, then add a third or a fourth of the avocado and a dollop of sour cream.

3. Fold as directed and serve at once.

Makes 3 or 4 servings.

FRESH SPINACH AND MUSHROOM OMELET

To complement the sprightly fresh green of the spinach that fills this omelet, add a garnish of tomato wedges and a fluff of alfalfa sprouts.

- ½ **pound mushrooms, thinly sliced**
- ¼ **cup finely chopped red onion**
- 3 **tablespoons butter or margarine**
- ¼ **teaspoon *each* salt and grated lemon rind**
- ⅛ **teaspoon *each* dried tarragon and ground nutmeg**
- 4 **cups lightly packed fresh spinach leaves**
  Basic Omelets (see page 37)
- 1 **small package (3 oz) cream cheese, cut in ½-inch cubes**

1. Cook mushrooms and onion in heated butter in a large frying pan over medium-high heat, stirring occasionally, until mushrooms are lightly browned. Mix in salt, lemon rind, tarragon, and nutmeg. Then add spinach, stirring over medium heat just until leaves are coated with mushroom mixture and beginning to wilt. Remove from heat.

2. Immediately prepare 3 or 4 Basic Omelets, following directions on page 37. Use a third or a fourth of the spinach and mushroom filling for each, dotting it with a third or a fourth of the cream cheese cubes.

3. Fold as directed and serve at once.

Makes 3 or 4 servings.

BRIE AND HAM OMELET

The warmth of a just-cooked omelet melts room-temperature Brie cheese so that its distinctive flavor spreads throughout, even though you won't need much of the cheese to fill several omelets. Accompany this brunch dish with a watercress and mushroom salad and a light red wine.

- ¼ **pound Brie cheese**
- 2 **tablespoons chopped shallots or mild onion**
- ¼ **pound thinly sliced baked ham or Black Forest ham, julienne cut**
- 6 **tablespoons butter or margarine**
- 2 **tablespoons chopped fresh parsley**
- ¼ **teaspoon dried tarragon**
  Basic Omelets (see page 37)

1. Let cheese stand at room temperature for about 1 hour to soften. Scoop cheese from rind, discarding rind, and set cheese aside.

2. Cook shallots and ham in 2 tablespoons of the butter in a medium frying pan over moderate heat, stirring occasionally until ham browns lightly and shallots are soft. Stir in parsley and tarragon. Keep warm while preparing omelets.

3. Prepare 3 or 4 Basic Omelets, following directions on page 37 and cooking them in remaining butter. Spoon dollops of cheese over each, using a third or a fourth of it. Then spoon a third or a fourth of the ham mixture over cheese on each omelet.

4. Fold as directed and serve at once.

Makes 3 or 4 servings.

CURRIED VEGETABLE OMELETS

Here is a meatless omelet with bold flavors. It is filled with toasted almonds and tender-crisp vegetables piquantly seasoned with curry powder. For breakfast or brunch add rye or whole wheat toast and freshly squeezed orange juice.

- 1 **cup small broccoli flowerets**
- ½ **cup thinly sliced carrots**
- 1 **medium onion, slivered**
- ¼ **cup finely chopped sweet red bell pepper**
- 2 **tablespoons butter or margarine**
- 1 **tablespoon olive oil or salad oil**
- ½ **teaspoon mustard seeds, slightly crushed**
- 1 **teaspoon curry powder**
- 1 **clove garlic, minced or pressed**
- ¼ **teaspoon ground cumin**
- ½ **teaspoon *each* salt and grated lemon rind**
  Basic Omelets (see page 37)
- 3 **to 4 tablespoons toasted sliced almonds**

1. Cook broccoli and carrots in a small amount of boiling salted water (or steam on a rack) until tender-crisp (4 to 6 minutes). Drain well and set aside.

2. In a medium frying pan, cook onion and red pepper in mixture of butter and oil with mustard seed and curry powder over medium heat, stirring frequently, until onion is soft but not brown. Mix in garlic, cumin, salt, lemon rind, and cooked vegetables. Keep warm.

3. Prepare 3 or 4 Basic Omelets, following directions on page 37. Use a third or a fourth of the curried vegetable filling for each, sprinkling each with about 1 tablespoon of the almonds.

4. Fold as directed and serve at once.

Makes 3 or 4 servings

STRAWBERRY BLINTZ OMELETS

This delicate omelet is filled with fluffy cream cheese and brown sugar and covered with fresh strawberries and sliced almonds. Accompany it with hot breakfast tea and warm brioches or toasted plain or sesame bagels.

- 1 basket (about 2 cups) strawberries
- 2 tablespoons Vanilla Sugar (see page 22)
- 1 small package (3 oz) cream cheese, softened
- 1 tablespoon milk or half-and-half (light cream)
  Pinch ground nutmeg
  Basic Omelets (see page 37 and Step 3 below)
- 3 to 4 tablespoons light brown sugar
- 3 to 4 tablespoons toasted sliced almonds

1. Hull strawberries, reserving a few with leaves for garnish; cut hulled berries in halves. Place in a bowl, mix lightly with Vanilla Sugar, and let stand at room temperature while preparing filling and omelets.

2. In a small bowl beat cream cheese with milk and nutmeg until fluffy.

3. Prepare 3 or 4 Basic Omelets, omitting pepper from egg mixture and following directions on page 37. Use a third or a fourth of the cream cheese mixture to fill each omelet, sprinkling cheese mixture in each with about 1 tablespoon of the brown sugar. Fold as directed.

4. Serve omelets on warm plates, spooning strawberries over and sprinkling each with about 1 tablespoon almonds. Serve at once.

Makes 3 or 4 servings.

COUNTRY VEGETABLE FRITTATA

Frittata is the Italian word for omelet, but a frittata differs in several ways from the preceding omelets. A frittata can be made in a larger pan and cut in wedges to serve several people. Although omelets are usually served as soon as they are cooked, a frittata can be eaten hot, lukewarm, or even cold. It is usually turned out before it has completed cooking, inverted, and returned to the frying pan to brown both sides. And the filling for a frittata becomes part of the egg mixture. This one, which in Italian is called *Frittata alla Contadina*, contains zucchini, carrot, herbs, onion, and peas. You might serve it with grilled Italian sausages and a crusty loaf of whole wheat bread.

- 1 medium zucchini
- 1 medium carrot, thinly sliced
- 8 eggs
- 3 tablespoons water
- ¼ teaspoon salt
  Dash *each* pepper and ground nutmeg
- 2 tablespoons grated Parmesan cheese
- 2 tablespoons *each* butter or margarine and olive oil
- ¼ cup thinly slivered onion
- 1 clove garlic, minced *or* pressed
- ¼ teaspoon dried oregano
- 2 tablespoons chopped fresh parsley
- ¼ cup thawed frozen peas

1. Cut zucchini into quarters, lengthwise; then cut crosswise into ¼-inch thick slices.

Cook carrots in a small amount of boiling salted water (or steam on a rack) until tender-crisp (4 to 6 minutes), adding zucchini for last 2 minutes of cooking time. Drain vegetables well and set aside.

2. Beat eggs in a large bowl with the 3 tablespoons water, salt, pepper, nutmeg, and Parmesan cheese.

3. Melt butter with 1 tablespoon of the oil in a well-seasoned or nonstick-coated 10- to 11-inch omelet pan over medium heat. Mix in onion and cook until limp. Add garlic, oregano, parsley, peas, and carrot mixture, stirring to coat with onions.

4. Pour egg mixture into pan and cook without stirring until it is set about ¼ inch around outer edge. With a wide spatula, lift some of the egg mixture from sides of pan, all the way around, tipping pan to let uncooked egg flow to pan bottom. Continue cooking until eggs are almost set but top of center is still moist and creamy.

5. Invert a large round flat plate (a little larger than frying pan) over pan. Holding plate and pan together, turn *frittata* out onto plate. Add remaining 1 tablespoon oil to pan, swirl to coat pan, then slide *frittata* from plate back into frying pan. Cook for about 2 minutes more to brown bottom lightly, then invert *frittata* onto a serving plate. Cut in wedges to serve.

Makes 4 servings.

While the Country Vegetable Frittata slowly cooks to golden perfection, sizzle Italian sausages on a grill for a hearty brunch.

BAKED EGGS

Baked —or shirred —eggs are easy to pre-pare, yet seem elegant when prepared in individual baking dishes. As the following recipes show, this style of egg cooking lends itself to many simple and delicious variations.

PARMESAN BAKED EGGS

In the basic recipe, eggs are baked in buttered shallow casseroles with Parmesan cheese. Following the variations, you can also bake the eggs in prosciutto-lined dishes, or after baking, sprinkle them with a savory selection of toppings.

- **2 tablespoons butter or margarine**
- **¼ cup grated Parmesan cheese**
- **4 eggs**
  Salt, ground nutmeg, and freshly ground pepper
  Chopped fresh Italian (flat-leaf) parsley, for garnish

1. Using about half of the butter, grease 4 shallow individual baking dishes about 5 inches in diameter. Coat each with 1 tablespoon of the Parmesan cheese.

2. Break an egg into each dish. Sprinkle lightly with salt, nutmeg, and pepper. Dot with remaining butter.

3. Bake, uncovered, in a 325°F oven until eggs are set to your liking (12 to 15 minutes). Sprinkle with parsley, then serve.

Makes 4 servings.

Prosciutto Baked Eggs: Do not coat baking dishes with Parmesan cheese. Instead, cook 4 thin slices prosciutto or other ham in butter until lightly browned, and line each baking dish with a prosciutto slice. Pour in any butter from frying pan. Continue as in basic recipe with eggs, salt, nutmeg, and pepper. Then sprinkle each egg with 1 tablespoon grated Parmesan cheese instead of dotting with butter.

Topping variations: After baking eggs, sprinkle with one or more of these toppings —thinly sliced green onions or snipped chives, red or green chile salsa, caviar, sour cream, crumbled crisp bacon, or shredded Swiss or sharp Cheddar cheese.

To flavor Parmesan Baked Eggs, you can add such toppings as green onions or chives, salsa, crumbled bacon, or shredded cheese. The recipe for Braided Egg Bread is on page 88.

TOMATO FRITTATA

A homemade tomato sauce, accented by basil, colors and flavors this lively frittata. Try it with French bread and artichokes vinaigrette.

- **1 small onion, finely chopped**
- **2 tablespoons olive oil**
- **1 clove garlic, minced or pressed**
- **1 can (1 lb) tomatoes**
- **1 teaspoon dried basil**
- **½ teaspoon salt**
- **⅛ teaspoon pepper**
- **6 eggs**
- **1 tablespoon finely chopped fresh parsley**
- **3 tablespoons butter or margarine**

1. Cook onion in olive oil in a medium frying pan until soft but not brown. Add garlic, tomatoes (coarsely chopped) and their liquid, basil, salt, and pepper. Bring to boiling, cover, reduce heat, and simmer for 10 minutes. Uncover and boil gently, stirring occasionally, until tomato mixture is thickened and reduced to about 1⅓ cups. Cool to room temperature.

2. Beat eggs in a large bowl; mix in tomato sauce and parsley. Melt 2 tablespoons of the butter in a 9-inch omelet pan over medium-low heat. Pour egg mixture into pan and cook, without stirring, until it is set about ¼ inch around outer edge. With a wide spatula, lift some of the egg mixture from sides of pan, all the way around, tipping pan to let uncooked egg flow to pan bottom. Continue cooking until eggs are almost set but top of center is still moist and creamy.

3. Invert a large round flat plate (a little larger than frying pan) over pan. Holding pan and plate together, turn frittata out onto plate. Add remaining 1 tablespoon butter to pan, swirl to melt butter, then slide frittata from plate back into frying pan. Cook for about 2 minutes more to brown bottom lightly, then invert frittata onto a serving plate. Cut in wedges to serve.

Makes 4 servings.

BAKED ARTICHOKE AND ONION FRITTATA

This frittata needs little attention, because it is baked in a casserole rather than being cooked on top of the range. Add crusty rolls and an avocado salad to complete the brunch menu.

- **1 package (9 oz) frozen artichoke hearts**
- **1 medium onion, slivered**
- **1 tablespoon *each* olive oil and butter or margarine**
- **¼ teaspoon dried oregano**
- **1 small clove garlic, minced or pressed**
- **¾ cup shredded Parmesan cheese**
- **6 eggs**
- **½ cup milk**
- **¼ teaspoon salt**
- **⅛ teaspoon *each* white pepper and ground nutmeg**
- **1 cup shredded Monterey jack cheese**

1. Cook artichoke hearts according to package directions until just tender; drain well.

2. In a medium frying pan cook onion in mixture of oil and butter over moderate heat until soft and beginning to brown. Mix in oregano, garlic, and artichokes. Remove from heat.

3. Generously grease a shallow 1½ to 2-quart round or oval casserole or baking pan. Coat sides and bottom with ¼ cup of the Parmesan cheese. Spoon artichoke mixture evenly over bottom.

4. Beat together eggs, milk, salt, pepper, and nutmeg. Mix in jack cheese and ¼ cup more of the Parmesan cheese. Pour over artichokes.

5. Bake, uncovered, in a 350°F oven for 30 minutes. Sprinkle evenly with remaining ¼ cup Parmesan cheese. Continue baking until frittata is puffed and golden brown (5 to 8 minutes).

Makes 4 servings.

SWISS BAKED EGGS

Baked eggs with a fonduelike flavor make an appealing breakfast for six, with French bread toast and *café au lait* or hot chocolate.

- ¼ **pound Swiss cheese, thinly sliced**
- 1 **green onion, thinly sliced**
- 1 **tablespoon chopped fresh parsley**
- 6 **eggs**
  Salt, ground nutmeg, and freshly ground pepper
- ¼ **cup whipping cream**
- 2 **tablespoons dry white wine**
  Toasted French bread slices

1. Line sides and bottom of a generously buttered, shallow 1½-quart baking dish (about 8 by 11 to 12 inches) with cheese. Sprinkle evenly with onion and parsley. Break eggs carefully into dish and sprinkle lightly with salt, nutmeg, and pepper.

2. In a medium bowl beat cream with wine just until well blended; pour around and between eggs.

3. Bake, uncovered, in a 325°F oven until eggs are set to your liking (12 to 18 minutes). Place eggs on hot, buttered, toasted French bread. Stir any melted cheese and cream remaining in baking dish until smooth, then spoon over eggs and toast.

Makes 6 servings.

BAKED EGGS IN TOMATO SAUCE

Accompany these Italian-style baked eggs with warm Italian or French bread and patties of homemade sausage (see page 49) if you wish.

- 1 **large onion, thinly slivered**
- ½ **pound mushrooms, thinly sliced**
- ¼ **cup chopped green pepper**
- ¼ **cup olive oil**
- 1 **clove garlic, minced or pressed**
- 1 **can (1 lb) tomatoes**
- ¼ **cup dry white wine**
- ⅓ **cup finely chopped fresh parsley**
- ½ **teaspoon *each* salt, ground cinnamon, and dried basil**
- ¼ **teaspoon *each* pepper and dried oregano**
- 6 **eggs**
- ½ **cup shredded Monterey jack cheese**

1. In a large frying pan cook onion, mushrooms, and green pepper in heated oil over medium heat, stirring frequently, until onions are soft and mushrooms are lightly browned. Mix in garlic, tomatoes (coarsely chopped) and their liquid, wine, parsley, and seasonings. Bring to boiling, cover, reduce heat, and simmer 10 minutes.

2. Uncover and boil gently, stirring occasionally, until tomato mixture is thickened and reduced to about 2½ cups. Transfer to a greased shallow 2-quart casserole. With the back of a spoon make 6 egg-size hollows. Break an egg into each.

3. Cover and bake in a 350°F oven for 12 minutes. Uncover, sprinkle with cheese, and continue baking until eggs are set to your liking and cheese melts (5 to 10 minutes).

Makes 6 servings.

SOUFFLÉS

Soufflés share with omelets an aura of sophistication—and have the edge on omelets for degree of difficulty. But like omelets, once you have learned the basics, you can make any soufflé. A dramatically puffed soufflé is such a hit for a brunch entrée that it is well worth mastering the really quite straightforward steps in creating one.

The basis for a soufflé is generally a fairly thick white sauce, to which may be added puréed or cooked vegetables or cheese—or some of each. Egg yolks are blended into the sauce. Then it is leavened with beaten egg whites. It is their expansion as the soufflé bakes that makes it rise and billow.

The only tricky part of preparing a soufflé has to do with the egg whites. First, they must be beaten enough but not too much—just until small, slightly curved peaks form. Then they must be folded lightly and carefully into the sauce just until incorporated, using a rubber spatula and a circular, up-and-over motion. Stirring in or overfolding the egg whites may release so much air that the soufflé will fail to rise.

Next comes baking. Be sure the oven is preheated before putting the soufflé inside. Don't open the door until the soffé is almost done. When it is ready, serve it at once! Sound advice for this delicate dish is to let your guests wait for the soufflé if need be, but never the other way around.

Timing the process is not as hard as you might think. You can make the sauce, up to the point of blending in the egg yolks, an hour or more before baking the soufflé. Just before baking, beat the egg whites and fold them in.

FOUR CHEESES SOUFFLE

An idea borrowed from the popular pasta sauce—combining four Italian-style cheeses—gives this soufflé a rich flavor. For brunch add a tomato salad with basil dressing and crusty rolls.

Butter or margarine
- 2 **tablespoons grated Parmesan cheese**
- 3 **tablespoons butter or margarine**
- 3 **tablespoons all-purpose flour**
  Dash cayenne
- ¼ **teaspoon *each* salt and dry mustard**
- ⅛ **teaspoon ground nutmeg**
- 1 **cup milk**
- ¼ **cup *each* crumbled Gorgonzola *or* other blue-vein cheese and diced Fontina cheese (¼-in. cubes)**
- ¾ **cup shredded Swiss cheese**
- 5 **eggs, separated**

1. Generously butter a 1½-quart soufflé dish and coat it evenly with the Parmesan cheese.

2. In a large, heavy saucepan melt the 3 tablespoons butter over medium heat. Stir in flour, cayenne, salt, mustard, and nutmeg; cook, stirring, until bubbly.

3. Remove from heat and gradually blend in milk. Return to heat and cook, stirring constantly, until thickened. Add Gorgonzola and Fontina cheeses and ½ cup of the Swiss cheese; stir until cheese melts. Remove pan from heat and beat in egg yolks, one at a time.

4. Beat egg whites until they form short, distinct peaks. Fold about half the whites thoroughly into the sauce, then gently fold in remaining whites. Pour into prepared soufflé dish. With the tip of a spatula, draw a circle around circumference of the soufflé about 1 inch in from side of dish. Sprinkle with remaining ¼ cup Swiss cheese.

5. Bake in a 350°F oven until soufflé is well browned and crust feels firm when tapped lightly (35 to 40 minutes). Serve at once.

Makes 4 servings.

SPINACH SOUFFLÉ

Puréed spinach gives this lavish soufflé an emerald color through and through. You might serve it with sliced roast turkey and buttery rolls.

- 1 **package (10 oz) frozen chopped spinach, thawed and well drained**
- ¼ **cup whipping cream *or* half-and-half (light cream)**
- ¼ **cup finely chopped shallots *or* mild onions**
- 3 **tablespoons butter or margarine**
- 2 **tablespoons all-purpose flour**
- ½ **teaspoon salt**
- ⅛ **teaspoon *each* ground nutmeg and dried tarragon**
  Pinch cayenne
- ¾ **cup milk**
- ½ **cup *each* shredded Swiss and Cheddar cheese**
- 5 **eggs, separated**

1. Place spinach in blender or food processor with cream and whirl or process until smooth.

2. In a large, heavy saucepan cook shallots in butter over medium heat, stirring occasionally, until soft but not brown. Stir in flour, salt, nutmeg, tarragon, and cayenne; cook, stirring, until bubbly.

3. Remove from heat and gradually blend in milk, then spinach purée. Return to heat and cook, stirring constantly, until thickened. Mix in cheeses, stirring until they melt. Remove pan from heat and beat in egg yolks, one at a time.

4. Beat egg whites until they form short, distinct peaks. Fold about half the whites thoroughly into the spinach mixture, then gently fold in remaining whites. Pour into a well buttered 1½-quart soufflé dish. With tip of a spatula, draw a circle around circumference of the soufflé about 1 inch in from side of dish.

5. Bake in a 350°F oven until soufflé is well browned and crust feels firm when tapped lightly (35 to 40 minutes). Serve at once.

Makes 4 servings.

MUSHROOM SOUFFLÉ WITH TARRAGON

Adding vegetables, such as finely chopped mushrooms, gives a traditional soufflé a new dimension of flavor.

6 tablespoons butter or margarine
1 shallot, finely chopped *or* 2 tablespoons finely chopped mild onion
6 ounces mushrooms, finely chopped
3 tablespoons all-purpose flour
Dash cayenne
¼ teaspoon dry mustard
⅛ teaspoon ground nutmeg
½ teaspoon *each* salt and dry tarragon
1 cup milk
1 cup shredded Gruyère *or* Swiss cheese
¼ cup chopped fresh parsley
5 eggs, separated

1. In a large, heavy saucepan melt butter over medium heat. Add shallot and mushrooms and cook, stirring often, until mushrooms brown lightly. Stir in flour, cayenne, mustard, nutmeg, salt, and tarragon. Cook, stirring, until bubbly.

2. Remove from heat and gradually blend in milk. Return to heat and cook, stirring constantly, until thickened. Add cheese and parsley and stir until cheese melts. Remove pan from heat and beat in egg yolks, one at a time.

3. Beat egg whites until they form short, distinct peaks. Fold about half of the whites thoroughly into the sauce, then gently fold in remaining whites. Pour into a well-buttered 1½-quart soufflé dish. With the tip of a spatula, draw a circle around circumference of the soufflé about 1 inch in from side of dish.

4. Bake in a 350°F oven until soufflé is well browned and crust feels firm when tapped lightly (35 to 40 minutes). Serve at once.

Make 4 servings.

INDIVIDUAL TOMATO SOUFFLES WITH BASIL AND SHRIMP

Here is a very special soufflé for a brunch main dish — it has a layer of savory tomato sauce and tiny shrimp hidden beneath its coral-colored body. Bake it either in individual soufflé dishes or in one large one.

1 medium onion, finely chopped
1½ tablespoons olive oil
1 clove garlic, minced or pressed
1 large can (28 oz) tomatoes
2 tablespoons fresh basil, coarsely chopped, *or* 1½ teaspoons dried basil
½ teaspoon sugar
1 teaspoon salt
¼ teaspoon pepper
¼ pound small peeled, cooked shrimp
2 tablespoons *each* butter or margarine and all-purpose flour
1 cup shredded Gruyère *or* Swiss cheese
5 eggs, separated

1. In a large saucepan cook onion in oil over medium heat until soft but not browned. Mix in garlic, tomatoes (coarsely chopped) and their liquid, basil, sugar, salt, and pepper. Bring to boiling, cover, reduce heat, and simmer for 15 minutes. Uncover and boil gently, stirring occasionally, until tomato mixture is thickened and reduced to about 1¾ cups.

2. Remove ½ cup of the tomato mixture, add shrimp to it, and divide mixture evenly among 4 well-buttered individual 1-cup soufflé dishes (or use a single 1½-quart soufflé dish); set dishes aside.

3. Place remaining tomato mixture in blender or food processor and whirl or process until smooth.

4. Melt butter in a large, heavy saucepan over medium heat. Stir in flour and cook, stirring, until bubbly. Remove from heat and gradually blend in tomato mixture. Return to heat and cook, stirring constantly, until thickened. Add ¾ cup of the cheese and stir until it melts. Remove pan from heat and beat in egg yolks, one at a time.

5. Beat egg whites until they form short, distinct peaks. Fold about half of the whites thoroughly into the tomato mixture, then gently fold in remaining whites. Divide mixture evenly among prepared soufflé dishes. With tip of a spatula, draw a circle around circumference of each soufflé about 1 inch in from side of dish. Sprinkle with remaining ¼ cup cheese.

6. Bake in a 350°F oven until soufflés are well browned and crust feels firm when tapped lightly (20 to 25 minutes for individual soufflés; 35 to 40 minutes for single soufflé in 1½-quart dish). Serve at once.

Makes 4 servings.

Once you have mastered the technique, it is easier than you might think to bake this spectacular fresh mushroom soufflé for a weekend brunch.

CALVADOS SOUFFLÉ

When you want a really elegant dessert to top off a brunch, consider this tender apple soufflé. It owes its flavor to Calvados (pronounce it CAHL-vah-dohs), a brash apple brandy from Normandy. But in the context of this soufflé and its custard sauce, the fire of the brandy is tamed to a sweet apple-scented warmth.

        Butter and sugar for soufflé dish
½   cup sugar
⅓   cup all-purpose flour
1⅓   cups milk
5   eggs, separated
1   teaspoon vanilla
¼   cup Calvados (French apple brandy)
2   teaspoons grated lemon rind
1   teaspoon grated orange rind
1¼   cups finely chopped tart green apples (peeled)
2   tablespoons butter or margarine
⅛   teaspoon cream of tartar
     Calvados Custard Sauce (recipe follows)

1. Generously butter a 1½- to 2-quart soufflé dish. Sprinkle with sugar, tipping and shaking to coat evenly. Set aside.

2. Mix the ½ cup sugar and the flour in a large, heavy saucepan. Using a whisk, gradually blend in milk, then egg yolks. Cook, stirring constantly, over medium heat until mixture thickens. Remove from heat and blend in vanilla, 2 tablespoons of the Calvados, and lemon and orange rinds.

3. In a medium frying pan cook apples in melted butter with remaining Calvados, stirring over medium heat until tender. Stir apples into egg yolk mixture. (This much can be done several hours ahead; cover lightly and let stand until ready to complete soufflé.)

4. Beat egg whites with cream of tartar until they form short, distinct peaks. Fold about half the whites thoroughly into apple mixture, then gently fold in remaining whites. Pour into prepared soufflé dish.

5. Bake soufflé, placing dish in a large, shallow pan filled to a depth of about 1 inch with hot water, in a 400°F oven for 25 to 30 minutes, until it is puffy and golden.

6. Serve at once, pouring Calvados Custard Sauce over each portion.

Makes 6 servings.

Calvados Custard Sauce: Scald ⅔ cup milk in top of double boiler over direct medium heat. Beat 2 egg yolks and 3 tablespoons sugar in a medium bowl, then gradually beat in scalded milk. Return milk mixture to double boiler over simmering water and cook, stirring constantly, until sauce begins to thicken and coats a metal spoon. Remove from heat and stir in 1 teaspoon vanilla and 2 tablespoons Calvados. Serve warm or cooled. Makes about 1 cup.

CHEESE-STUFFED BAKED GREEN CHILIES

Not as tricky as a soufflé, this *chiles rellenos*-like casserole is delicious for brunch with warm, buttered tortillas and grilled sausages.

1   large can (7 oz) green chilies
½   pound Monterey jack *or* longhorn cheese
1   medium onion, finely chopped
3   tablespoons all-purpose flour
½   teaspoon baking powder
⅛   teaspoon salt
3   eggs, separated

1. Slit chilies and carefully remove seeds. Cut cheese into as many strips as there are chilies. Fill chilies with cheese strips and chopped onion; reshape chilies to cover filling. Place them in a single layer in a greased 8-inch-square baking pan or shallow 2-quart casserole.

2. Mix flour, baking powder, and salt. Add 1 tablespoon of the egg whites to the egg yolks, then beat egg whites until stiff but not dry. Using the same beater, beat egg yolks until light colored, then beat in flour mixture. Mix in a little of the beaten egg whites to lighten mixture, then fold beaten egg whites into egg yolk mixture. Pour batter over stuffed chilies.

3. Bake in a 325°F oven for 20 to 30 minutes, until batter is set and top is golden brown. Serve at once.

Makes 4 to 6 servings.

ROULADE WITH MUSHROOM FILLING

A *roulade* is a soufflé-like mixture baked in a large flat pan, then rolled up, jelly-roll fashion, around a filling. Serve these light, moist, mushroom-swirled slices for brunch with a crisp green salad, French bread, and a dry white wine.

     Butter or margarine for baking pan
¼   cup butter or margarine
¼   cup all-purpose flour
     Pinch *each* ground nutmeg and cayenne
½   teaspoon salt
¾   cup milk
6   eggs, separated
¼   teaspoon cream of tartar
     Mushroom Filling (recipe follows)
3   tablespoons grated Parmesan cheese
½   cup shredded Gruyère *or* Swiss cheese

1. Butter a 15- by 10-inch shallow baking pan, line bottom with waxed paper, and butter it generously.

2. Melt the ¼ cup butter in a medium saucepan over medium heat. Mix in flour, nutmeg, cayenne, and salt; cook, stirring, until bubbly. Remove from heat and gradually blend in milk. Cook, stirring constantly, until mixture thickens and pulls away from sides of pan.

3. Using a wire whisk, beat egg yolks in a large bowl. Gradually blend in thickened sauce. In another large bowl beat egg whites with cream of tartar until stiff peaks form. Fold egg whites into egg yolk mixture. Spread in prepared pan.

4. Bake in a 350°F oven until roulade is puffy and surface is firm when pressed lightly (15 to 20 minutes).

5. Invert onto a large sheet of aluminum foil on a baking sheet. Peel off waxed paper. Spread evenly with Mushroom Filling; sprinkle with Parmesan cheese. Starting from a long edge, roll up carefully. Place roll in center of foil. Sprinkle top with Gruyère cheese.

6. Broil, about 4 inches from heat, until cheese is melted and lightly browned (3 to 4 minutes). Slice and serve at once.

Makes 4 to 6 servings.

Mushroom Filling: Finely chop ¾ pound mushrooms. Melt ¼ cup butter or margarine in a large frying pan over medium-high heat. Add mushrooms and ¼ cup *each* finely chopped shallots or mild onion and finely chopped ham. Cook, stirring, until liquid is gone and mushrooms brown lightly. Stir in ¼ teaspoon *each* salt and dried tarragon and ¼ cup whipping cream. Cook, stirring, until most of the liquid is gone. Makes about 1¾ cups.

A dry white wine complements this mushroom-filled roulade. The delicate, soufflé-like roll first is baked, then filled and rolled. It is finished with a sprinkling of Gruyère cheese and a few minutes beneath the broiler.

Bring home the bacon—or the ham, sausages, even ground beef, chicken, and fish. All are fine choices for breakfast and brunch variety.

MORNING MEATS, POULTRY AND FISH

When you think of a hearty breakfast to linger over, it's probably a combination of a savory meat with eggs: crisp strips of bacon with eggs sunny-side up or nuggets of ham scrambled with creamy eggs. These classics have earned a deserved place on anyone's morning menu. But there is no reason to stop with these. Variety is welcome on a daily basis, for a family Sunday breakfast, and certainly for a brunch.

If you are at all adventurous, why limit yourself to such safe but predictable options as ham, bacon, or sausage? Enjoy the novelty of fish for breakfast: crisply baked stuffed trout or tangy smoked fish in the curried rice dish the English have dubbed Kedgeree. Or such shellfish as scallops and oysters in delicate brunch dishes.

Consider the morning meal as a time for employing leftovers creatively: corned beef in a wonderfully fresh-tasting hash, with or without poached eggs; creamed turkey in crusty, hollowed-out French rolls.

Potatoes, for many, go with meat whenever possible—even at breakfast. That's why this chapter includes a special feature on the kinds of potatoes one craves in the morning: hashed browns, cottage fries, and crisp skins.

For those who feel better knowing *exactly* what goes into their food, there is the option of making bulk pork sausage. It doesn't take long and requires little more equipment than a food chopper or processor. You can freeze what you don't need at the moment.

Shape homemade Bulk Pork Sausage (the recipe is on page 49) into small patties to sauté and savor for breakfast with Cheddar Cheese Muffins (page 84).

To make Joe's Special, add eggs to a savory scramble of well-browned ground beef with onion, mushrooms, and fresh spinach. With a loaf of crusty bread you'll have a sure-fire brunch success.

JOE'S SPECIAL

Ground beef for brunch! Why not? Especially when it is browned quickly with onion and mushrooms, then scrambled with spinach and eggs to make a longtime San Francisco favorite—Joe's Special. Serve with a crusty loaf of bread, butter, and a light red wine such as an Italian or California Barbera or Grignolino.

- 1 pound ground beef, crumbled
- 1½ tablespoons olive oil or salad oil
- 1 large onion, finely chopped
- 1 clove garlic, minced or pressed
- ¼ pound mushrooms, sliced
- 1 teaspoon salt
- ⅛ teaspoon *each* pepper and oregano
  Pinch ground nutmeg
- 2 cups coarsely chopped fresh spinach
- 3 eggs
  Grated Parmesan cheese

1. Brown ground beef well in heated oil in a large frying pan over high heat.

2. Add onion, garlic, and mushrooms; reduce heat and continue cooking, stirring occasionally, until onion is soft. Stir in seasonings and spinach; cook for about 5 minutes longer, stirring several times, until spinach is limp.

3. Reduce heat to low and break eggs over meat mixture; quickly stir just until eggs begin to set. Serve immediately, with cheese to sprinkle over each serving to taste.

Make 3 to 4 servings.

BREAKFAST POTATOES

Go ahead, indulge! Once in a while prepare one of these irresistible potato side dishes to complement sausage, ham, or bacon with eggs. The Hashed Brown Potatoes are grated, then crisply fried with a touch of onions. Give Cottage Fried Potatoes a down-home appeal by cooking, slicing, and frying them with the well-scrubbed skins on. Baked Potato Skins are delicious as is, or as containers for scrambled or poached eggs.

HASHED BROWN POTATOES

  **5 medium potatoes (about 2 lbs)
  Salted water
  ¼ cup finely chopped onion
  ½ teaspoon salt
  Pinch white pepper
  2 tablespoons *each* butter or
  margarine and salad oil**

1. Cook potatoes, in their jackets, in boiling salted water until about half cooked (15 to 20 minutes). When cool enough to handle, slip off skins. Shred potatoes coarsely into a bowl. Mix lightly with onion, salt and pepper.

2. Melt butter with 1 tablespoon of the oil in a heavy, well-seasoned or nonstick 9- to 10-inch frying pan over medium heat. Add potatoes, pressing down with a spatula. Cook over low heat (without stirring) until potatoes are brown and crusty on bottom (12 to 15 minutes).

3. Loosen edges with a spatula. Cover pan with a large plate, invert potatoes onto it, and add remaining 1 tablespoon oil to pan. Swirl to coat pan well. Slide potatoes back into pan and cook until bottom is well browned and crusty (12 to 15 minutes).

4. Serve from pan or invert onto a warm serving plate.

Makes 6 servings.

COTTAGE FRIED POTATOES

  **5 medium potatoes (about 2 lbs)
  Salted water
  2 tablespoons *each* butter or
  margarine and salad oil
  ⅛ teaspoon paprika
  Salt and coarsely ground
  pepper**

1. Scrub potatoes well. Cook, in their jackets, in boiling salted water until about half cooked (15 to 20 minutes). Without peeling, slice potatoes about ⅛ inch thick.

2. Melt butter with oil and paprika in a large, heavy frying pan over medium-low heat. Add potatoes, sprinkling lightly with salt and pepper.

3. Cook, using a wide spatula to lift and turn potatoes occasionally, until they are brown and crusty on all sides (20 to 25 minutes). Turn carefully to keep slices from breaking.

Makes 4 to 6 servings.

BAKED POTATO SKINS

  **6 small baking potatoes
  (4 to 5 in. long)
  ¼ cup butter or margarine
  ¼ teaspoon paprika
  Pinch white pepper**

1. Scrub potatoes, pat dry, and rub skins lightly with a little of the butter. Pierce each potato in several places with a fork.

2. Bake potatoes in a 400°F oven until tender when pierced (45 minutes to 1 hour). When cool enough to handle, cut potatoes in halves and scoop out potato, leaving a thin shell about ⅛ inch thick. Reserve scooped-out potato for other dishes (see Fisherman's Pie, page 57).

3. Place potato skins in a single layer on a baking sheet. Melt butter in a small pan with paprika and pepper, stirring to combine. Brush insides of potato skins with butter mixture.

4. Bake potato skins in a 400°F oven until crisp and golden (18 to 20 minutes). (If you wish, serve with shredded Cheddar cheese, crumbled crisp bacon, and/or thinly sliced green onion or chives.)

Makes 6 servings.

CUSTARDY BAKED SAUSAGE SANDWICHES

This fine family Sunday brunch dish must be assembled ahead and refrigerated—for as long as 24 hours if you wish—in order to become puffy and crisply crusted when it is baked. Try it with crisp raw vegetables on crushed ice and a tart fruit sherbet for dessert.

  **8 slices cracked wheat bread
  Coarse-grained Dijon mustard
  1 pound bulk pork sausage,
  crumbled
  1 small onion, finely chopped
  1 cup shredded Swiss cheese
  4 eggs
  ½ cup sour cream
  ¾ teaspoon salt
  Pinch *each* white pepper and
  ground nutmeg
  2 cups milk
  Paprika**

1. Trim crusts from bread if you wish. Spread half of the slices lightly with mustard. Place, mustard sides up, in a well-buttered 8- or 9-inch-square baking dish.

2. Cook sausage and onion in sausage drippings in a medium frying pan over medium heat, stirring occasionally, until sausage is lightly browned. Using a slotted spoon, spoon sausage mixture evenly over bread slices in baking dish. Sprinkle evenly with cheese. Cover with remaining bread slices.

3. In a medium bowl, beat eggs with sour cream, salt, pepper, and nutmeg. Gradually beat in milk until well blended. Pour egg mixture slowly and evenly over top bread slices. Sprinkle lightly with paprika. Cover and refrigerate for at least 1 hour (or as long as overnight if you wish).

4. Bake, uncovered, in a 325°F oven until sandwiches are puffed and custard is set in center (45 minutes to 1 hour).

Makes 4 servings.

Custardy Baked Sausage Sandwiches and grapefruit juice combine for a winning Sunday family brunch.

BULK PORK SAUSAGE

- 2 pounds boneless pork butt, cut in 1-inch cubes
- 1 clove garlic, minced or pressed
- 1½ teaspoons dried sage
- 1 teaspoon salt
- ½ teaspoon *each* dried summer savory *or* marjoram and coarsely ground black pepper
- ¼ teaspoon *each* ground allspice and dried thyme
- ⅛ teaspoon cayenne pepper

1. Using coarse blade of food chopper, grind pork cubes twice. *Or*, to use food processor for grinding meat, first spread pork cubes in a single layer on a baking sheet and place in freezer until meat is firm but not frozen (about 20 minutes). Then process, using short on-off bursts, until meat is coarsely ground.

2. Using mortar and pestle or blender, combine garlic and seasonings thoroughly. Add to ground meat and mix well until seasonings are evenly distributed. (Use your hands if you wish.)

3. Wrap well and refrigerate for 8 hours or overnight to blend flavors.

4. Form into patties and cook in a frying pan over medium-low heat until well browned and crusty on both sides, or use in recipes as directed.

Makes 2 pounds.

GRILLED ITALIAN SAUSAGES WITH PEPPERS

In fair weather or foul, these sausages —grilled outdoors on the barbecue or indoors in a frying pan—make a satisfying brunch with Italian or French bread, and omelets rolled around Fontina or Parmesan cheese.

- 1½ pounds Italian sausages
- 2 tablespoons *each* butter or margarine and olive oil
- 1 large onion, thinly slivered
- 1 *each* sweet red and green bell pepper, seeded and cut in thin strips
- 1 small clove garlic, minced or pressed
- ½ teaspoon *each* salt and dried oregano
  Freshly ground black pepper
  Lemon wedges and Italian (flat-leaf) parsley, for garnish

A colorful sauté of onion and sweet red and green peppers is delicious with both grilled Italian sausages and individual cheese-filled omelets.

1. Pierce each sausage in several places with a fork. Place on grill about 6 inches above a bed of glowing coals. (Or cook on a range-top grill or in a large, heavy frying pan over medium-low heat.) Cook, turning occasionally, until well browned and cooked in center (20 to 25 minutes). (Juice should run clear when a sausage is pierced with a fork.)

2. While sausages are cooking, melt butter with oil in a large frying pan over medium heat. Add onion, and cook, stirring often, until limp. Mix in peppers, garlic, salt, and oregano. Continue cooking until onions brown lightly and peppers are tender-crisp (about 5 minutes). Grind pepper over mixture to taste.

3. Spoon pepper mixture in center of a warm platter; surround with cooked sausages. Garnish with lemon and parsley.

Makes 4 to 6 servings.

KAREN'S HAM AND SPINACH ROLLS

Here is an easy and very elegant brunch dish that will serve 8 to 10. Thinly sliced ham is rolled around a filling that combines spinach, sour cream, and cornbread stuffing mix. Topped with a robust cheese sauce, it can be made ahead, refrigerated, then baked later. As accompaniments, serve a molded carrot and pineapple salad, sesame seed rolls, and if wine is in order, a crisp, dry rosé.

- **2 packages (10 oz *each*) frozen chopped spinach, thawed**
- **2 cups sour cream**
- **¼ teaspoon ground nutmeg**
- **2 cups packaged cornbread stuffing mix**
- **20 thin slices (about 1¼ lbs) baked *or* boiled ham**
- **Nippy Cheese Sauce (recipe follows)**
- **½ cup grated Parmesan cheese**

1. Drain spinach in a colander, pressing out moisture. In a large bowl stir together spinach, sour cream, and nutmeg. Blend in stuffing mix.

2. Place about ¼ cup of the spinach mixture on each ham slice, rolling them up and placing side-by-side in a buttered shallow 3-quart baking dish (about 9 by 13 inches).

3. Pour cheese sauce evenly over ham rolls. Sprinkle with Parmesan cheese. If made ahead, cover and refrigerate.

4. Bake, covered, in a 350°F oven for 15 minutes. Uncover and bake until sauce is bubbly and lightly browned (15 to 20 minutes; add 5 to 10 minutes to baking time if made ahead).

Makes 8 to 10 servings.

Nippy Cheese Sauce: Melt 2 tablespoons butter or margarine in a medium saucepan over moderate heat. Stir in 2 tablespoons all-purpose flour and ⅛ teaspoon cayenne pepper; cook until bubbly. Remove from heat and gradually blend in 1½ cups milk. Return to heat and cook, stirring, until thickened and bubbling. Stir in 1 cup shredded sharp Cheddar cheese until melted, then mix in 1 tablespoon dry sherry. Makes about 2 cups.

Bake this cheese-sauced casserole, Karen's Ham and Spinach Rolls, just long enough to brown the top lightly. Serve for brunch with salad and rolls.

DILLED CORNED BEEF HASH

Buttery browned onions aplenty make this homemade corned beef hash an irresistible dish with rye toast and mugs of strong, steaming coffee.

- **½ cup butter or margarine**
- **2 large onions, finely chopped**
- **½ teaspoon sugar**
- **2 medium potatoes, cooked, peeled, and diced**
- **3 to 4 cups cooked corned beef brisket, cut in ½-inch cubes**
- **½ teaspoon dried dillweed**
- **⅛ teaspoon pepper**
- **4 to 6 warm poached eggs (optional; see page 32)**
- **Fresh dill sprigs *or* chopped fresh parsley, for garnish**

1. Melt half of the butter in a large, heavy frying pan over medium heat until foamy. Add onions and sugar; cook slowly, stirring occasionally, until onions are soft and golden (about 20 minutes).

2. Swirl in 2 tablespoons more of the butter, then lightly mix in potatoes, corned beef, dillweed, and pepper. Press mixture down lightly with a spatula. Cook over medium heat until bottom of hash is golden brown when an edge is lifted with spatula (about 10 minutes).

3. Loosen hash with spatula. Cover pan with a large plate (wider than pan) and invert hash onto plate. Add remaining 2 tablespoons butter to pan and swirl until melted. Slide hash back into pan, browned side up. Continue cooking slowly until bottom is golden brown (10 to 15 minutes).

4. Again invert hash onto warm plate. If you wish, use a spoon to make 4 to 6 hollows in hash and slip a poached egg into each. Garnish with dill or parsley.

Makes 4 to 6 servings.

SWEETBREADS AND MUSHROOMS IN MARSALA CREAM

Spoon these rich creamed sweetbreads over toasted English muffins. Or if you wish to be a bit fancier, bake puff pastry patty shells to hold the sweetbreads. If you like, this can be a buffet dish, served from a chafing dish *bain marie*.

- **1½ pounds sweetbreads**
- **1½ teaspoons salt**
- **Water**
- **2 tablespoons lemon juice**
- **¼ cup butter or margarine**
- **½ pound mushrooms, thinly sliced**
- **2 tablespoons all-purpose flour**
- **⅛ teaspoon *each* white pepper and ground nutmeg**
- **¾ cup chicken broth, homemade or canned**
- **1 cup half-and-half (light cream)**
- **1 egg yolk**
- **2 tablespoons dry *or* sweet Marsala wine**
- **6 English muffins, split, toasted, and buttered**
- **Watercress sprigs, for garnish**

1. Place sweetbreads in a large, heavy saucepan; sprinkle with 1 teaspoon of the salt. Add water to cover by about 1 inch and 1 tablespoon of the lemon juice. Bring to boiling over medium heat, then reduce heat and simmer, covered, for 15 minutes.

2. Drain sweetbreads, place in a bowl, and cover with cold water. Let stand until cool, changing water several times. Drain and pat dry. Use a small knife to peel membranes and cut out connecting tubes. Separate sweetbreads into bite-size pieces. (You should have about 3 cups.)

3. In a large frying pan, brown sweetbreads lightly in 2 tablespoons of the butter over medium heat, removing and reserving sweetbreads as they brown. When all are browned, add remaining butter to pan. In it cook mushrooms until lightly browned. Stir in flour, remaining ½ teaspoon salt, pepper, and nutmeg and cook until bubbly. Remove from heat and gradually blend in broth and half-and-half.

4. Return to heat and cook, stirring, until thickened and bubbling, then boil gently for 5 minutes. Beat egg yolk in a small bowl; blend in a little of the hot mushroom sauce. Then add egg yolk mixture to remaining mushroom sauce. Cook, stirring, over low heat until thickened and smooth. (Do not boil.)

5. Blend in remaining 1 tablespoon lemon juice and Marsala, then add sweetbreads. Stir gently just until sweetbreads are heated through.

6. Spoon sweetbreads over hot, toasted muffins. Garnish with watercress.

Makes 6 servings.

TAILGATE BRUNCH

Bloody Marys (see page 19)
Ham in Rye Buns with Mustard Sauce
Crisp Raw Vegetables Mixed Pickles
Shredded Apple Cake   Pears Coffee

Arrive at the stadium early enough to avoid parking hassles, and you will have plenty of time before an afternoon game for a late-morning brunch. Yeasty homemade rye rolls filled with ground ham make an unusual hot sandwich.

To serve them hot on game day, take either approach: bake the rolls a day or more ahead and refrigerate or freeze them; reheat, lightly covered, in a 325°F oven, then wrap well to stay hot. Or, shape the rolls the night before, cover lightly and refrigerate, then bake in the morning. Carry the hot sauce in a wide-mouth thermos.

HAM IN RYE BUNS WITH MUSTARD SAUCE

- 1 **package active dry yeast**
- 1 **cup hot water**
- ¼ **cup sugar**
- ½ **teaspoon salt**
- ½ **cup butter or margarine, softened**
- 3 **cups all-purpose flour**
- 1 **egg**
- ½ **cup rye flour**
   Ground Ham Filling (recipe follows)
- ¼ **cup salad oil**
   Dilled Mustard Sauce (recipe follows)

1. Sprinkle yeast over water in the large bowl of an electric mixer; let stand about 5 minutes to soften. Stir in sugar, salt, and butter, mixing until butter melts. Add 2½ cups of the all-purpose flour. Mix to blend, then beat 5 minutes at medium speed. Beat in egg, then vigorously mix in remaining ½ cup all-purpose flour and rye flour until well combined.

2. Place batter in a greased bowl, cover, and let rise in a warm place until doubled in bulk (about 1 hour). Punch down, turn dough out on a generously floured board or pastry cloth, and roll to a 16- by 12-inch rectangle. Cut dough into twelve 4-inch squares. Place about ¼ cup filling in center of each square. Bring opposite corners together and pinch to seal.

3. Measure 1 teaspoon oil into each of twelve 2½-inch muffin cups. Place each square of filled dough in a muffin cup and turn to coat with oil, ending with pinched side down.

4. Let rise until buns are puffy (45 minutes to 1 hour). Bake in a 400°F oven until well

Spread out on the tailgate for a late-morning brunch are ham-filled rye rolls, served warm with crisp raw vegetables, followed by a homemade apple cake.

browned (20 to 25 minutes). Serve hot with Dilled Mustard Sauce.

Makes 12 servings.

Ground Ham Filling: Cook 1 small onion (finely chopped) in 2 tablespoons butter or margarine in a medium frying pan until soft but not brown. Mix in 1 clove garlic (minced or pressed), and cook for 1 minute longer. Remove from heat and mix in 3 cups ground cooked smoked ham, ½ cup sour cream, and ¼ teaspoon ground cloves.

Dilled Mustard Sauce: In a heavy, medium-size saucepan melt ¼ cup butter or margarine over medium heat. Mix in 3 tablespoons all-purpose flour, ½ teaspoon *each* salt and dried dillweed, and ⅛ teaspoon white pepper. Cook, stirring, until bubbly. Remove from heat and blend in 1 tablespoon Dijon mustard, then gradually stir in 2 cups milk. Cook, stirring constantly, until thickened and boiling. Beat 1 egg yolk in a small bowl; gradually blend in a little of the hot sauce. Blend egg yolk mixture into remaining hot sauce. Add 2 tablespoons lemon juice and return to low heat. Cook, stirring, just until thickened and smooth. (Do not boil.) Makes about 2⅓ cups.

SHREDDED APPLE CAKE

- ½ **cup butter or margarine, softened**
- 2 **cups sugar**
- 1 **teaspoon vanilla**
- 2 **eggs (at room temperature)**
- 2 **cups all-purpose flour**
- 1½ **teaspoons baking soda**
- ½ **teaspoon ground nutmeg**
- 1 **cup finely chopped walnuts**
- 2 **tart apples, peeled, cored, and shredded**
   Whipped cream (optional)

1. In a large bowl cream butter, sugar, and vanilla until fluffy. Add eggs, one at a time, beating well after each addition.

2. Mix flour, soda, and nutmeg. Add half the flour mixture to butter mixture and beat well. Gradually mix in remaining flour, beating well after the last addition. Fold in nuts and apples.

3. Spread batter in a well greased, lightly floured 8½- to 9-inch bundt pan or other 9-cup tube pan.

4. Bake in a 325°F oven for 1 hour and 10 to 15 minutes, until cake tests done when a long skewer is inserted in thickest part. Let cool in pan for 10 minutes, then invert cake onto a wire rack.

5. Serve warm or cool, with whipped cream if you wish.

Makes 1 cake (8 to 10 servings).

Lamb Cakes, topped with colorful pimientos and parsley, make a good brunch accompaniment to meatless quiches, crêpes, or omelets.

3. Cover and bake in a 325°F oven for about 1 hour, until chicken and vegetables are tender. Uncover and bake for 10 to 15 minutes longer, until chicken is brown and crisp.

4. Spoon vegetables and sauce over chicken before serving.

Makes 4 servings.

CHICKEN TARRAGON-FILLED BRIOCHES

For those who enjoy baking, the quick buttery brioches on page 87 make a fine medium for this creamy chicken, but it can also be served over fluffy rice. If you make the chicken sauce in advance, cover and refrigerate it; then reheat, stirring gently, in a double boiler over simmering water.

- 3½- to 4-pound frying chicken, cut up
  Salt, white pepper, and nutmeg
- 3 tablespoons butter *or* margarine
- ¼ cup finely chopped shallots *or* mild onion
- 1½ teaspoons dried tarragon
- ⅓ cup chopped fresh parsley
- 1½ cups dry white wine
- ¾ cup whipping cream
- 1 egg yolk
- 6 warm brioches (see recipe, page 87)
- 1 avocado, peeled and cut in wedges, for garnish
  Cherry tomatoes, for garnish

1. Sprinkle chicken pieces lightly with salt, white pepper, and nutmeg. Brown chicken lightly on all sides in heated butter in a large, heavy frying pan.

2. Add shallots, tarragon, parsley, and wine. Bring to boiling, cover, reduce heat, and simmer for 1 hour, until chicken is very tender. Remove chicken and reserve cooking liquid in pan.

3. Remove chicken from bones, discarding skin and bones; cut into bite-size pieces.

4. Add cream to cooking liquid and bring to boiling. Boil, stirring occasionally, until reduced by about a fourth. Remove from heat. Beat egg yolk in a small bowl; blend a little of the hot liquid with yolk, then return all to pan. Mix in chicken. Cook, stirring lightly, over low heat until sauce thickens slightly. (Do not boil after adding egg yolk.) Taste, and add salt if needed.

5. Cut brioches to—but not through— bottom crusts into quarters; spread open carefully on individual plates. Spoon hot chicken mixture into brioches. Garnish with avocado wedges and cherry tomatoes.

Makes 6 servings.

LAMB CAKES

If, for brunch, you would like to accompany a vegetable omelet, quiche, or crêpes with a somewhat offbeat meat, try these ground lamb patties. They are served with a colorful hot garnish of pimientos and parsley.

- 1 egg
- ¼ cup soft bread crumbs
- ½ teaspoon garlic salt
- ⅛ teaspoon cinnamon
- 1 jar (4 oz) pimientos, drained and finely chopped
- 1 pound ground lean lamb
- 1 tablespoon *each* butter or margarine and olive oil
- 1 teaspoon lemon juice
- 1 tablespoon water
- ¼ cup chopped fresh parsley

1. In a medium bowl beat egg slightly, then mix in crumbs, garlic salt, cinnamon, and ¼ cup of the chopped pimientos. Lightly mix in lamb; shape mixture into 8 flat patties.

2. Brown lamb patties slowly over medium heat in mixture of butter and oil in a large frying pan, turning once and cooking about 6 minutes on each side. Remove patties to a warm serving dish and keep them warm.

3. Pour off and discard all but about 1 tablespoon of the pan drippings. Add remaining pimientos, lemon juice, water, and parsley. Cook, stirring to incorporate brown bits from pan, just until mixture is heated through. Spoon over lamb patties.

Makes 4 servings.

YANKEE CLIPPER CHICKEN

Accompany this hearty New England brunch dish with fluffy homemade biscuits and honey.

- 3 to 3½-pound frying chicken, cut in quarters
  Salt, white pepper, ground nutmeg, and all-purpose flour
- 1 tablespoon *each* butter or margarine and salad oil
- 4 carrots, sliced ¼ inch thick
- 1 onion, thinly sliced
- ½ cup chopped celery
- ¼ cup *each* chicken broth and dry vermouth *or* dry sherry

1. Sprinkle chicken lightly on all sides with salt, pepper, and nutmeg; then coat lightly with flour, shaking off excess. Melt butter with oil in a large, heavy frying pan over medium heat; in it brown chicken well on all sides. As chicken browns, remove quarters and place in a single layer, skin sides up, in a 10-inch-square casserole.

2. Pour off and discard all but about 1 tablespoon of the drippings. Add carrots, onion, and celery; cook, stirring, until onion is tender and lightly browned. Add chicken broth and vermouth; stir to incorporate pan drippings. Pour vegetable mixture over chicken.

MAPLE BAKED CHICKEN

The slightly sweet flavor of this baked chicken, topped with crispy almonds, makes it a good choice for brunch with rice and fresh peas.

- ¼ **cup butter or margarine**
- **3-pound frying chicken, cut up**
- ¼ **cup slivered blanched almonds**
- ¼ **cup maple syrup**
- 1 **teaspoon salt**
  Dash *each* **ground nutmeg and white pepper**
- ½ **teaspoon grated lemon rind**
- 2 **teaspoons lemon juice**

1. While heating oven to 350°F, place butter in a shallow baking dish and heat in oven until butter is melted and bubbling.

2. Place chicken pieces, skin sides down, in melted butter; then turn skin sides up. Sprinkle chicken with almonds. Combine maple syrup with remaining ingredients; pour evenly over chicken.

3. Bake, uncovered, for about 1 hour, drizzling occasionally with cooking liquid, until chicken is well browned and tests done at thickest parts.

Makes 4 to 5 servings.

LEMONY CREAMED TURKEY IN FRENCH ROLLS

Hollow out and toast rectangular or round French rolls to make containers for this delicious turkey, caper, and ripe olive filling. Add cranberry-orange relish for a sweet-sour flavor contrast.

- 4 **sourdough French rolls, about 5½ by 3½ inches, or 4 inches in diameter**
- ½ **cup butter or margarine**
- 1 **teaspoon lemon juice**
- ⅛ **teaspoon paprika**
- 1 **small clove garlic, minced or pressed (optional)**
- 3 **green onions, thinly sliced (use part of tops)**
- 3 **tablespoons all-purpose flour**
- ½ **teaspoon salt**
  Pinch white pepper
- 1½ **cups half-and-half (light cream)**
- 1 **teaspoon Dijon mustard**
- ⅔ **cup dry white wine**
- 2 **cups diced cooked turkey**
- ⅓ **cup sliced ripe olives**
- 1 **tablespoon drained capers**
- 1 **teaspoon grated lemon rind**
  Thinly sliced green onions, for garnish

1. Cut off tops of French rolls, then scoop out each bottom to make a ½-inch-thick case. (Save tops and insides to use for bread crumbs in other recipes.) Melt

Split homemade brioches and fill them with creamy chicken seasoned with tarragon. The recipe is on the previous page.

¼ cup of the butter in a small pan with lemon juice, paprika, and garlic (if used). Brush insides of rolls with butter mixture and place on a baking sheet.

2. Bake, uncovered, in a 325°F oven until rolls are crisp and insides are golden brown (20 to 25 minutes). Keep warm.

3. In a large, heavy saucepan melt remaining ¼ cup butter over medium heat. Add the 3 sliced green onions and cook just until limp. Stir in flour, salt, and white pepper; cook, stirring, until bubbly.

4. Remove flour mixture from heat and gradually blend in half-and-half and mustard. Cook, stirring until thickened.

5. Blend in wine, then mix in turkey, olives, capers, and lemon rind. Cook, stirring occasionally, a few minutes longer until heated through.

6. To serve, spoon creamed turkey evenly into and over warm, toasted French rolls. Sprinkle with sliced green onions.

Makes 4 servings.

TURKEY HASH WITH CURRY SAUCE

A good post-holiday brunch dish, this hash tastes fine with a molded cranberry salad and your favorite rolls.

- 1 **medium onion, thinly slivered**
- 1 **small sweet red** *or* **green bell pepper, seeded and finely chopped**
- ¼ **cup butter or margarine**
- ¼ **teaspoon paprika**
- 4 **cups diced cooked turkey**
- 1 **medium potato, cooked, peeled, and diced**
- ¼ **cup golden raisins**
- ½ **teaspoon salt**
  Pinch white pepper
  Curry Sauce (recipe follows)

1. In a 10-inch frying pan cook onion and red or green pepper in heated butter over medium heat, stirring until soft but not brown. Mix in paprika.

2. Lightly mix in turkey, potato, raisins, salt, and pepper. Press down lightly with a spatula. Continue cooking over medium heat until hash is heated through and a golden brown crust forms on bottom (10 to 12 minutes).

3. Loosen hash with a spatula. Cover pan with a warm serving plate (larger than the pan), and invert hash onto plate. Serve hash with sauce.

Makes 4 to 6 servings.

Curry Sauce: In a medium saucepan melt 2 tablespoons butter over medium heat. Stir in 1 teaspoon curry powder, then 2 tablespoons all-purpose flour, and ¼ teaspoon *each* salt and dry mustard. Cook, stirring, until bubbly. Remove from heat and gradually blend in 1 cup chicken broth and ¾ cup milk. Add ½ teaspoon grated lemon rind. Cook, stirring constantly, until thickened; then cook, stirring occasionally, for 2 minutes. Makes about 2 cups.

To make the most of kippered salmon, combine it with curried rice in Kedgeree. Serve for brunch with toast and tea.

KEDGEREE

This curiously named Anglo-Indian creation combines curry-seasoned rice, smoked salmon or haddock (finnan haddie), and hard-cooked eggs to make an irresistible brunch dish. Indigenous flavors that seem to team naturally with Kedgeree are those of breakfast tea and toast with tomato preserves or marmalade.

- **1 small onion, finely chopped**
- **¼ cup butter or margarine**
- **¾ teaspoon curry powder**
- **1 cup long grain *or* California pearl rice**
- **½ teaspoon salt**
- **2 cups water**
- **¾ pound kippered salmon *or* haddock**
- **2 tablespoons all-purpose flour Pinch white pepper**
- **1½ cups chicken broth, canned or homemade**
- **3 hard-cooked eggs (see page 29) Finely chopped fresh parsley, for garnish**

1. In a large, heavy frying pan cook onion in 2 tablespoons of the butter over medium heat until soft but not brown. Stir in curry powder and rice until well combined. Sprinkle with salt. Add water, cover, reduce heat, and simmer until rice is tender and liquid is absorbed (20 to 25 minutes).

2. Steam fish on a rack over gently boiling water until it separates easily into flakes (10 to 15 minutes). Flake fish, reserving a few large pieces for garnish; keep warm.

3. In a medium saucepan melt remaining 2 tablespoons butter over moderate heat.

Add flour and pepper, stirring until bubbly. Remove from heat and gradually blend in chicken broth. Cook, stirring, until thickened and boiling. Then boil gently, stirring occasionally, until reduced to about 1 cup.

4. Cut eggs in halves. Shred yolks and whites separately.

5. Into the cooked rice mix flaked fish and sauce. Spoon into a warm serving dish. Top with reserved pieces of fish and shredded eggs. Sprinkle with parsley.

Makes 4 to 6 servings.

BROILED KIPPERS WITH SWEET-SOUR ONIONS

Sturdy British breakfasts often include these smoked, salted fish, dotted with butter and broiled in a jiffy. Suitable accompaniments are tomato halves broiled (along with the kippers) with herb butter, toast, and an English breakfast tea.

- **2 kippered herring (*each* about 6 oz), butterflied Boiling water**
- **1 large onion, thinly sliced and separated into rings**
- **3 tablespoons butter or margarine**
- **½ teaspoon mustard seeds, coarsely crushed**
- **1 teaspoon sugar**
- **1 tablespoon raspberry *or* red wine vinegar Freshly ground black pepper**

1. To remove some of the salt, place herring in a baking dish, pour on boiling water to cover, and let stand for 10 to 15 minutes. Drain herring and pat dry.

2. Cook onion in 2 tablespoons of the butter over moderately low heat in a large frying pan until limp. Stir in mustard seeds and sugar and continue cooking, stirring occasionally, until onions are golden (about 10 minutes).

3. Place herring, opened out, with skin sides down, on rack of broiler pan, and dot with remaining 1 tablespoon butter. Broil, about 4 inches from heat, until fish are hot and bubbling (6 to 8 minutes). (It is not necessary to turn fish.)

4. Just before serving, add vinegar to onions, stirring to deglaze the pan and reduce most of the liquid. Divide onions between each of 2 warm plates. Place a broiled herring beside onions on each plate. Sprinkle pepper over all.

Makes 2 servings.

BAKED STUFFED TROUT

This is a delicious fisherman's breakfast, starring freshly caught brook trout. But even if you are not a sportsman and must rely on a fish market for the trout, it still makes a delicious morning meal.

- **1 medium onion, finely chopped**
- **1 stalk celery, finely chopped**
- **¼ cup butter or margarine**
- **1 clove garlic, minced or pressed**
- **½ teaspoon salt**
- **¼ teaspoon dried tarragon**
- **⅛ teaspoon lemon pepper**
- **¼ cup finely chopped fresh parsley**
- **3 cups cubed firm bread**
- **1 egg**
- **1 tablespoon dry white wine**
- **4 whole trout (about 8 oz *each*), cleaned Salt**
- **1 tablespoon *each* lemon juice and soy sauce All-purpose flour**
- **2 slices bacon, cut in halves crosswise**

1. In a large frying pan cook onion and celery in butter over medium heat until soft and lightly browned. Remove from heat and mix in garlic, salt, tarragon, pepper, parsley, and bread. Beat egg with wine; mix lightly with bread mixture. Spread evenly in a shallow buttered baking dish just large enough to hold trout.

2. Wipe trout, inside and out, with a damp paper towel. Sprinkle with salt. Mix lemon juice and soy sauce; brush cavities of trout with mixture. Coat trout lightly with flour; arrange over stuffing. Drizzle with any remaining soy-lemon mixture. Cover each fish with a half-slice of bacon.

3. Cover and bake in a 350°F oven for about 45 minutes, until fish are firm. Uncover and continue baking until bacon is crisp and brown (10 to 15 minutes).

Makes 4 servings.

If you like fish in the morning, you can't beat Baked Stuffed Trout with warm corn sticks. Summer-fresh berries with cream and sugar bring the brunch to a delightful conclusion.

CRUSTY OYSTER GRATIN

In a wintry "R" month, serve these butter-crusted baked oysters for brunch with a marinated broccoli salad, hard rolls, a dry white wine such as Muscadet, and a hot apple or pear dessert.

- ½ cup (¼ lb) butter or margarine
  Pinch *each* dried thyme and cayenne pepper
- 2 jars (10 oz *each*) small oysters
- 1 cup finely crushed soda cracker crumbs
- 2 tablespoons finely chopped fresh parsley

1. Melt butter with thyme and cayenne in a small frying pan.

2. Drain oysters and pat dry. Sprinkle a well-buttered, shallow 1½- to 2-quart baking dish evenly with half of the cracker crumbs. Dip oysters into melted butter mixture to coat. Arrange oysters in a single layer over crumbs in baking dish. Sprinkle with parsley, then cover with remaining cracker crumbs. Drizzle with butter remaining in frying pan.

3. Bake, uncovered, in a 400°F oven until crumbs are crisp and brown (15 to 18 minutes).

Makes 4 servings.

SCALLOPS IN TOMATO CREAM

Baked in scallop shells or ramekins, scallops with the Provençal touch of a creamy fresh tomato sauce make an unexpected brunch entrée. Serve them with rice or a loaf of good bread and a delicate green salad.

- 1 pound scallops, thawed if frozen
- ¼ cup butter or margarine
- ¼ cup finely chopped shallots *or* mild onion
- ½ pound mushrooms, thinly sliced
- 1 large tomato, peeled and chopped
- 1 teaspoon tomato paste
- ⅓ cup dry white wine
- ½ teaspoon *each* salt and dried tarragon
- ⅛ teaspoon white pepper
- ½ cup whipping cream
- 2 tablespoons chopped fresh parsley
- ½ cup shredded Gruyère cheese

1. Brown scallops lightly in butter in a large frying pan over medium-high heat, removing them as they brown and dividing them evenly into 4 buttered baking shells or shallow individual casseroles.

2. In same pan cook shallots and mushrooms, stirring frequently, until shallots are tender and mushrooms brown lightly. Mix in tomato, tomato paste, wine, salt, tarragon, and pepper. Bring to boiling, cover, reduce heat, and simmer 10 minutes.

3. Uncover, stir in cream, and bring to boiling over high heat. Cook, stirring, until sauce is reduced and slightly thickened. Remove from heat and mix in parsley. Spoon sauce over scallops. Sprinkle evenly with cheese.

4. Bake in a 400°F oven until sauce bubbles and begins to brown at edges (about 10 minutes).

Makes 4 servings.

Scallops in Tomato Cream, baked in individual shells, are a brunch treat. Serve them with fluffy rice to spoon alongside, and a delicate green salad.

SHAD ROE WITH CAPER BUTTER

Shad roe, the pouch-shaped eggs of a saltwater fish that spawns in coastal rivers, is a spring treat for those who appreciate its delicate flavor and unique texture. It makes an elegant breakfast for two, served on toast triangles in a simple lemon, caper, and butter sauce with a fine dry white wine. You might go all out and make the wine Champagne. Curls of crisply fried bacon or frizzled ham also taste good with the fish.

- 1 set (about ¾ lb) shad roe
  Salt, white pepper, and all-purpose flour
- ¼ cup butter or margarine
- 1 tablespoon *each* lemon juice and drained capers
  Buttered toast triangles
  Lemon wedges and parsley sprigs, for garnish

1. Rinse shad roe (without separating the 2 halves if possible) and pat dry. Sprinkle with salt and pepper, then coat lightly with flour.

2. Melt 2 tablespoons of the butter in a medium frying pan over medium heat. Add shad roe and cook, turning once, until roe are nicely browned on both sides and look opaque. (Test center of each half with a small knife.) Remove from pan, separate into halves, and keep warm.

3. To pan add remaining 2 tablespoons butter and lemon juice, swirling and stirring in pan drippings until mixture bubbles. Mix in capers.

4. Place roe on toast triangles on warm plates, pour caper butter over, and garnish with lemon wedges and parsley.

Makes 2 servings.

LOBSTER PIE

This "pie" is really a sherried lobster casserole baked with a topping of crisp crumbs. Use crab in place of lobster if you wish. For brunch, add buttered whole green beans and whole wheat or bran muffins.

- 3 tablespoons butter or margarine
- ¼ cup finely chopped onion
- 3 tablespoons all-purpose flour
- ¼ teaspoon *each* salt and paprika
  Pinch white pepper
- 2 cups half-and-half (light cream)
- 2 tablespoons dry sherry
- 1 teaspoon Worcestershire sauce
- 1 tablespoon lemon juice
- 2 tablespoons chopped fresh parsley
- 1 pound (about 3 cups) cooked lobster *or* crabmeat
  Bread Crumb Topping (recipe follows)

1. Melt butter in a heavy 2- to 3-quart saucepan over medium heat. Stir in onion

and cook until soft but not browned. Stir in flour, salt, paprika, and pepper; cook until bubbling. Remove from heat and gradually blend in half-and-half, then sherry. Return to medium-low heat and cook, stirring constantly, until boiling and thickened.

2. Fold in Worcestershire sauce, lemon juice, parsley, and lobster. Spread in a buttered shallow 5- to 6-cup casserole. Sprinkle evenly with Bread Crumb Topping.

3. Bake, uncovered, in a 400°F oven until bread crumbs are brown and crisp (15 to 20 minutes).

Makes 4 servings.

Bread Crumb Topping: In a small frying pan melt 2 tablespoons butter or margarine with ⅛ teaspoon paprika. Stir in 1½ cups soft bread crumbs.

HANGTOWN FRY

Dating back to California Gold Rush days, this classic Western oyster, bacon, and egg dish is a sort of frittata.

- **6 slices bacon, cut in halves**
- **¼ cup butter or margarine**
- **1 jar (10 oz) small oysters**
- **6 eggs**
   All-purpose flour
- **⅓ cup fine dry bread crumbs**
- **1 tablespoon water**
- **½ teaspoon salt**
   Pinch white pepper
- **1 tablespoon finely chopped fresh parsley**

1. In a 10-inch nonstick-coated frying pan cook bacon until crisp and brown; remove bacon, drain, and keep warm. Discard bacon drippings. To pan add 3 tablespoons of the butter, swirling until melted.

2. While bacon cooks, drain oysters and pat dry. Beat 1 of the eggs in a medium bowl. Coat oysters first with flour, then with egg, and finally with bread crumbs. Add oysters to melted butter in pan and cook over medium-low heat until brown on first side. Turn to brown second side.

3. As oysters brown, to egg in which oysters were dipped add remaining 5 eggs, water, salt, and pepper. Beat until frothy and well combined (about 30 seconds). After turning oysters, sprinkle with parsley then pour beaten eggs into frying pan.

4. Cook as for a frittata (see page 39), lifting and tipping pan as eggs begin to set. When eggs are nearly set, cover pan with a large plate, invert eggs and oysters onto it, and add remaining 1 tablespoon butter to pan. Swirl until melted. Slide eggs back into pan and cook until bottom is lightly browned.

5. Cut in wedges and serve from pan, or invert onto a warm serving plate and cut in wedges. Accompany with bacon.

Makes 4 servings.

Lightly cooked oysters nestle into a bacon-topped frittata to become Hangtown Fry, a fine brunch dish.

FISHERMAN'S PIE

Mounds of cheese-crusted mashed potatoes give this creamy seafood combination — salmon and tiny shrimp — the air of a seafaring shepherd's pie. If fresh salmon fillet is not available, canned salmon (drained and flaked) will serve.

- **4 medium potatoes (about 1½ lbs)**
   Salted water
- **1 pound salmon fillets**
- **¼ pound mushrooms, thinly sliced**
- **¼ cup butter or margarine**
   Creamy Sauce (recipe follows)
- **½ cup thawed frozen peas**
- **¼ cup chopped fresh parsley**
- **¼ pound tiny peeled, cooked shrimp**
- **¼ teaspoon salt**
   Pinch *each* white pepper and ground nutmeg
- **2 to 3 tablespoons milk *or* cream**
- **1 cup shredded Cheddar cheese**

1. Peel potatoes and cut lengthwise into quarters. Cook in boiling salted water until tender (about 20 minutes).

2. Place salmon on a rack above about ½ inch of water in a medium frying pan. Bring water to boiling, cover, reduce heat, and steam until salmon flakes when tested with a fork (6 to 8 minutes). Separate salmon into bite-size chunks, removing and discarding any bones or skin.

3. In a medium frying pan cook mushrooms in 2 tablespoons of the butter until lightly browned.

4. Into Creamy Sauce fold salmon, mushrooms, peas, parsley, and shrimp. Spread in a buttered shallow 2- to 2½-quart baking dish.

5. Drain cooked potatoes well. Add remaining 2 tablespoons butter, salt, pepper, and nutmeg. Beat, adding milk gradually, until potatoes are fluffy. Spread potatoes lightly around edges of fish mixture in casserole, *or* drop potatoes by small spoonfuls, *or* pipe through a pastry bag, using a large star tip. Sprinkle cheese evenly over all. (If made ahead, cover and refrigerate.)

6. Bake, uncovered, in a 400°F oven, until potatoes brown lightly and sauce is bubbling (20 to 30 minutes).

Makes 6 servings.

Creamy Sauce: In a large, heavy saucepan melt 3 tablespoons butter or margarine over medium heat. Stir in 3 tablespoons all-purpose flour, ¼ teaspoon salt, and a pinch *each* white pepper and nutmeg; cook until bubbling. Remove from heat and gradually mix in 2 cups half-and-half (light cream); cook, stirring, until thick. Boil gently, stirring occasionally, for 2 minutes. Mix in ⅔ cup shredded Swiss cheese until melted. Makes about 2½ cups.

A stack of buttery pancakes means "Sunday morning" in many homes. For a change in routine, try waffles, crêpes, oven pancakes, blintzes, and blini.

THE PANCAKE AND WAFFLE FAMILY

Hot off the griddle—the very phrase suggests an irresistible freshness. Perhaps that is why pancakes, waffles, French toast, and similar creations from other cultures—crêpes, blintzes, blini—are so popular for breakfasts and brunches.

All contain some flour and many are classified as quick breads. But such variations as crêpes and billowy oven pancakes are also very eggy, giving them a certain delicacy.

Many of these pancakelike breakfast treats require a special pan or iron to give them a distinctive shape or imprint. You will find descriptions of these attractive and desirable utensils on page 61.

Every culture has a favorite kind of pancake, some made in a particular kind of pan. The recipe for these diminutive and delicate Swedish Pancakes is on page 60, and there's more about the pan on page 61.

PANCAKES

The easy way to make pancakes is from a mix. But if you do, you will miss some of the appealing flavors and textures that can be added only during step-by-step preparation. Actually, pancake batter is quite simple—a mixture of flour with a bit of sugar and leavening, added to beaten egg, milk, and a little shortening. For quick breakfasts, you can have the dry ingredients combined, all ready to stir into the egg mixture. Do this while your griddle is heating.

If you purchase a new pancake griddle, season it with oil before using. The procedure is the same as seasoning an omelet pan (see page 6). As with an omelet pan, a well seasoned pancake griddle should not be washed after using. Wipe away any clinging bits with a little oil and a paper towel, and store the griddle in a dry place.

On a fine summer Sunday morning, take Blueberry Yogurt Pancakes and maple syrup outdoors to savor in a shaded nook on the porch or patio.

BLUEBERRY YOGURT PANCAKES

These puffy hotcakes are made with a combination of plain yogurt and milk. They are dotted with fresh or frozen blueberries and are delicious with butter and maple syrup.

- 1 cup all-purpose flour
- 1 tablespoon sugar
- 1 teaspoon baking powder
- ½ teaspoon baking soda
- ¼ teaspoon salt
- ⅛ teaspoon ground nutmeg
- 1 egg
- ½ cup *each* plain yogurt and milk
- 2 tablespoons salad oil
- ¾ cup fresh *or* unsweetened frozen blueberries
- Butter or margarine and maple syrup

1. Stir together flour, sugar, baking powder, soda, salt, and nutmeg. Beat egg with yogurt and milk in a large bowl. Beat in oil, then add flour mixture. Stir just until combined. (Batter can be a little lumpy.)

2. Grease seasoned pancake griddle if necessary, and place over medium heat until a few drops of water dance on the hot griddle. Using a scant ¼ cup batter for each pancake, pour batter onto the hot griddle. Sprinkle each pancake with several blueberries.

3. Cook pancakes on first side until they are puffed, full of bubbles, and look dry at edges. Then turn and cook until second side is golden brown. Serve at once with butter and syrup.

Makes about twelve 4-inch pancakes (3 to 4 servings).

BANANA HOTCAKES WITH HONEY-PECAN BUTTER

Mashed fresh banana makes these special pancakes moist and flavorful. The toasted pecan and honey butter is a delicious flavor complement and can replace syrup on other favorite hotcakes.

    1 cup all-purpose flour
    2 teaspoons baking powder
    ½ teaspoon salt
    ⅛ teaspoon ground nutmeg
    2 tablespoons sugar
    1 egg
    1 cup milk
    3 tablespoons salad oil
    1 cup mashed bananas
    2 teaspoons lemon juice
       Honey-Pecan Butter (recipe
       follows)

1. Stir together flour, baking powder, salt, nutmeg, and sugar. Beat egg with milk in a large bowl. Beat in oil, then bananas and lemon juice. Add flour mixture. Stir just until combined. (Batter can be a little lumpy.)

2. Grease seasoned pancake griddle if necessary, and place over medium heat until a few drops of water dance on the hot griddle. Using a scant ¼ cup batter for each hotcake, pour batter onto hot griddle.

3. Cook hotcakes on first side until they are puffed, full of bubbles, and look dry at edges. Then turn and cook until second side is golden brown. Serve at once with Honey-Pecan Butter.

Makes sixteen to eighteen 3½-inch hotcakes (4 to 6 servings).

Honey-Pecan Butter: Spread ⅓ cup pecans in a shallow pan. Toast in a 350°F oven for about 8 minutes; cool. Chop toasted pecans finely. In a medium bowl beat ½ cup softened butter or margarine until fluffy; beat in ¼ cup honey until well combined. Then mix in chopped pecans. If made ahead, cover and refrigerate. Let stand at room temperature to soften before serving. Makes about 1 cup.

SWEDISH PANCAKES

These moist, delicate little pancakes are a specialty of Little River Inn, a welcoming hostelry on the northern California coast near Mendocino. Serve them in the Swedish manner, with butter and lingonberry preserves—or with your favorite syrup. The pancakes require a special pan, described on page 61.

    ⅔ cup all-purpose flour
    ½ teaspoon *each* sugar and
       baking powder
    ⅛ teaspoon salt
    2 eggs, separated
    1 cup milk
    ¼ cup half-and-half (light cream)
    ¼ cup butter or margarine, melted
       and cooled
       Butter or margarine and
       lingonberry preserves *or* syrup

1. Stir together flour, sugar, baking powder, and salt. Beat egg yolks with milk and half-and-half in a large bowl. Beat in melted butter, then add flour mixture. Stir to combine. (Batter will be slightly lumpy.)

2. Beat egg whites until stiff but not dry. Fold into batter.

3. Place lightly oiled Swedish pancake pan (see page 61) over medium-low heat until a few drops of water dance on the hot surface. Add about 2 tablespoons of the batter for each pancake. Cook pancakes until golden brown on each side, turning once.

4. Serve hot with butter and lingonberry preserves or syrup.

Makes twenty-five 3-inch pancakes (4 to 6 servings).

GINGERBREAD PANCAKES WITH LEMON SAUCE

The enticing sauce for these spicy griddlecakes is tart, clear, warm, and lemony. Add homemade sausage patties (see page 49) for a Sunday family breakfast.

    1⅓ cups all-purpose flour
    1 teaspoon baking powder
    ¼ teaspoon *each* baking soda and
       salt
    ½ teaspoon ground ginger
    1 teaspoon ground cinnamon
    1 egg
    1¼ cups milk
    ¼ cup molasses
    3 tablespoons salad oil
       Lemon Sauce (recipe follows)

1. Stir together flour, baking powder, soda, salt, ginger, and cinnamon. Beat egg with milk in a large bowl. Beat in molasses, then oil. Add flour mixture and stir just until combined. (Batter can be a little lumpy.)

2. Grease seasoned pancake griddle if necessary, and place over medium heat until a few drops of water dance on the hot griddle. Using a scant ¼ cup batter for each pancake, pour batter onto hot griddle.

3. Cook pancakes on first side until they are puffed, full of bubbles, and look dry at edges. Then turn and cook until second side is browned. Serve at once with hot Lemon Sauce.

Makes about eighteen 3½-inch pancakes (4 to 6 servings).

Lemon Sauce: In a medium saucepan mix ½ cup sugar, 1 tablespoon cornstarch, and a pinch ground nutmeg. Gradually mix in 1 cup hot water. Cook, stirring, over medium heat until mixture is thick and clear. Add 2 tablespoons butter or margarine, ½ teaspoon grated lemon rind, and 2 tablespoons lemon juice, stirring until butter melts. Serve hot. Makes about 1⅓ cups.

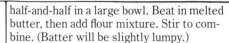

A good change from the usual syrup is this fluffy Honey-Pecan Butter —delicious with fruity Banana Hotcakes. Add fruit and tea for a weekend breakfast.

SPECIAL PANS FOR SPECIAL PANCAKES

Some of the most fascinating utensils in the cookware world are designed to produce uncommon pancakes, waffles, and the like. Some are even handsome enough to adorn a kitchen wall. If you enjoy varying your breakfast and brunch repertoire, you will probably want to add one or more of these to your cupboards.

The first to consider is a crêpe pan. *It resembles an omelet pan in that it is fashioned of rolled steel. A closer look shows that it differs in one important respect —the crêpe pan has a flat, well defined bottom (to give the crêpe a sharp edge) and flaring sides. The sides of an omelet pan, on the other hand, curve gently into the bottom.*

Season a new crêpe pan as you would an omelet pan (see page 6). Reserve it strictly for crêpes and you will never need to wash it. Just use a little oil and a paper towel to wipe away any clinging crumbs after each use, then store the pan in a dry place to prevent rust. Rub a little oil over the sides and bottom as it heats before you make the next batch of crêpes.

Crêpe pans range in size from about 5 to 8½ inches (diameter of the crêpe or pan bottom, not the top edge). Most of the crêpe recipes in this book specify 6- to 7-inch crêpes.

A Breton crêpe griddle *is notable for its large size —11 or 12 to 15 inches in diameter. It is not as deep as smaller crêpe pans, with just a shallow, upturned rim to contain the flowing crêpe batter. Made of cast aluminum or cast iron, it also can be used as a griddle for modest domestic pancakes and grilled sandwiches, as well as the thin, eggy Breton-style crêpes.*

A blini pan, *by contrast, is so small some people mistake it for a one-egg frying pan. It has a bottom diameter of 3½ to 4 inches to shape the diminutive Russian pancakes. Aside from its modest size, it is very like a standard crêpe pan in design and should be seasoned and cared for in the same way.*

Special pancake and waffle pans shown are (clockwise from lower left): heart-shaped waffle iron, large Breton crêpe griddle, Belgian waffle iron, Swedish pancake pan, croque monsieur iron from France, and standard crêpe pan. Blini pan is in center.

A Swedish pancake pan, *made for the delicate, eggy pancakes for which a recipe is given on page 60, can also be used to make blini. In one respect it is even more convenient, because you can make several pancakes at a time. The pan is a large (about 10 inches in diameter) cast iron griddle containing 7 shallow, 3-inch-round depressions. Season and treat it as you would any other cast iron pan (see page 6).*

Another attractive Scandinavian utensil is the heart-shaped waffle iron. *Circular, its cast iron grids consist of 5 interlocking hearts. Range-top irons must be turned once as the waffles bake.*

From France or Belgium comes the inspiration for the cast aluminum Belgian waffle iron. *(Some are imported and others made in the United States.) You can find them both plain and with nonstick coatings. They differ from conventional irons in gridding a waffle with deeper pockets to hold more syrup or other topping.*

Also French is the croque monsieur *iron, a cast aluminum sandwich grill. It toasts your breakfast sandwich while imprinting it with a cockleshell pattern. Somehow the charming design makes even a peanut butter sandwich taste elegant.*

The last two, as well as crêpe pans, can be ordered from: Williams-Sonoma, Mail Order Department, P.O. Box 3792, San Francisco, California 94119.

All are available as range-top utensils, and can be used on both gas and electric surface units. More sophisticated electric versions of some are made, but this refinement is really not necessary to a successful product.

QUICK BUCKWHEAT BLINI

A yeast-leavened batter gives blini —Russian appetizer pancakes—a tartness that complements the flavor of the buck-wheat flour in them. They make a splendid brunch main dish with ice-cold vodka or Champagne or dry white wine.

- **1   package active dry yeast**
- **¼   cup warm water**
- **¾   cup milk**
- **½   teaspoon sugar**
- **¼   teaspoon salt**
- **¼   cup butter or margarine, softened**
- **¾   cup all-purpose flour**
- **¼   cup buckwheat flour**
- **1   egg, separated**
       Melted butter, sour cream, caviar or smoked salmon, and lemon wedges and chopped hard-cooked egg

1. In large bowl of an electric mixer, sprinkle yeast over warm water. Let stand until softened (about 5 minutes).

2. Heat milk in a medium saucepan until steaming; remove from heat and mix in sugar, salt, and butter, stirring until butter melts. Let stand until cooled to lukewarm. Stir into yeast mixture, then add all-purpose and buckwheat flours and egg yolk. Mix to blend, then beat until smooth (1 to 2 minutes).

3. Cover bowl and let stand in a warm place until batter is doubled and slightly sour smelling (about 1 hour). Stir batter down. Beat egg white until stiff. Fold egg white into batter and let stand for about 10 minutes.

4. Using 2 to 3 tablespoons batter for each, bake blini in lightly oiled, preheated 4½- to 5-inch blini pan or in each depression of Swedish pancake pan (see page 61) until crisp and golden brown on each side, turning when tops are bubbly and look dry at edges.

5. Keep blini warm in a 250°F oven until they are all baked, then serve topped with melted butter, sour cream, and caviar or smoked salmon, accompanied by lemon wedges and chopped hard-cooked egg.

Makes 15 to 20 blini (3 to 4 servings).

SPINACH BRUNCH PANCAKES

If you have a Swedish pancake pan you can also use it to make these diminutive Scan-dinavian spinach cakes for a brunch. Offer a choice of such toppings as melted butter, sour cream, and red caviar or smoked salm-on. As accompaniments, serve a tomato salad with dill dressing and beer or white wine.

- **1½ cups milk**
- **2   eggs**
- **½   teaspoon *each* salt and sugar**
- **⅛   teaspoon ground nutmeg**
- **1   cup all-purpose flour**
- **2   tablespoons butter, melted and cooled**
- **1   package (10 oz) frozen chopped spinach, thawed, well drained, and squeezed dry**
       Butter or margarine
       Melted butter, sour cream, and red caviar or smoked salmon

1. In food processor using plastic blade (or mixing bowl) combine milk, eggs, salt, sugar, nutmeg, and flour. Process (or beat in bowl) until smooth, stopping motor once or twice to stir flour from sides of container.

2. Add melted butter and spinach; process (or stir) until well combined.

3. For each pancake melt a little butter in 4½- to 5-inch blini pan or in each depres-sion of Swedish pancake pan (see page 61) over medium heat until bubbling. Add about 2 tablespoons of the spinach batter for each pancake, spreading to cover pan bottom (or individual depressions of Swedish pancake pan). Cook pancakes until lightly browned on each side, turning once. Add a bit more butter for later pancakes.

4. Keep baked pancakes warm on a heatproof serving platter in a 250°F oven. Serve topped with melted butter, sour cream, and red caviar or smoked salmon.

Makes 20 to 24 pancakes (about 6 servings).

Make Basic Crêpes (see page 63) or the Dessert Crêpes (see page 67), and sprinkle with sugar and grated orange rind while crêpes are warm. Then spoon Hot Buttered Plums (recipe on page 23) over each serving, and present as a brunch dessert.

CRÊPES

In their country of origin, France, crêpes are served as a snack, a lunch or supper dish, or—depending on flavoring and embellishment—dessert. But that is no reason not to enjoy them for breakfast and brunch.

Filled and sauced in a variety of ways, then baked just before serving, crêpes are the ideal main dish to prepare in advance for a friendly get-together.

You can make basic crêpes that serve well for most main dishes, or sweeten them slightly for dessert. Variations such as main-dish crêpes made with whole wheat or buckwheat flour or with cornmeal are also possible.

BASIC CRÊPES

Here is the recipe for the plain main-dish crêpes used in several recipes. If you wish, they can be made ahead and frozen, then thawed and filled later.

    1   cup all-purpose flour
    ¾   cup water
    ⅔   cup milk
    3   eggs
    2   tablespoons salad oil
    ¼   teaspoon salt

1. In blender or food processor combine all ingredients. Whirl or process until batter is smooth, stopping motor once or twice to scrape flour from sides of container.

2. Cover and refrigerate batter for at least 1 hour. Blend batter well before making crêpes.

3. Make crêpes (see column at right) using a lightly oiled 6-inch pan. Stack them as each crêpe is completed.

Makes 16 to 20 crêpes.

CHICKEN AND SPICED APPLE CRÊPES

For brunch, try this subtly sweet crêpe combination with whole green beans and a dry Gewürztraminer.

    5   tablespoons butter or
        margarine
    2   medium-size tart cooking
        apples, peeled and coarsely
        shredded
    1   teaspoon *each* sugar and lemon
        juice
    ¼   teaspoon ground cinnamon
    ⅛   teaspoon *each* ground
        coriander and nutmeg
    3   to 3½ cups chopped Simmered
        Chicken (directions follow)
    3   tablespoons all-purpose flour

    ¼   teaspoon salt
        Dash white pepper
    ¾   cup chicken broth
    1   cup half-and-half (light cream)
    1   egg yolk
   16   Basic Crêpes, 6 to 7 inches in
        diameter
    1   tablespoon dry white wine
    ¼   cup sliced almonds

1. Melt 2 tablespoons of the butter in a medium frying pan over moderate heat. Stir in apples and cook until just tender, stirring often. Mix in sugar, lemon juice, cinnamon, coriander, and nutmeg. Fold in chicken and set mixture aside.

2. Melt remaining 3 tablespoons butter in a medium saucepan over moderate heat. Stir in flour, salt, and white pepper; cook until bubbling. Remove from heat and gradually blend in chicken broth and half-and-half. Cook, stirring constantly, until thickened. Beat egg yolk in a small bowl; blend in a little of the hot sauce, then blend mixture, off heat, into remaining sauce. Cook, stirring over low heat, just until thickened (1 to 2 minutes). Fold about a third of the sauce into chicken-apple mixture.

3. Fill crêpes, dividing chicken mixture evenly, and roll them up. Place side by side in a shallow buttered baking dish about 9 by 13 inches.

4. Blend wine into remaining sauce; pour evenly over crêpes. Sprinkle with almonds. (If made ahead, cover and refrigerate.)

5. Bake, uncovered, in a 425°F oven until crêpes are heated through and sauce is lightly browned (12 to 15 minutes; 20 to 25 minutes if refrigerated).

Makes 8 servings.

Simmered Chicken: Cut up a 3- to 3½ pound frying chicken. Place chicken pieces in a 4½- to 5-quart Dutch oven or deep frying pan. Add ½ teaspoon salt, ⅛ teaspoon dried thyme, ⅛ teaspoon whole peppers (white or black), 3 sprigs fresh parsley, 1 stalk celery (chopped), and 3 cups water. Bring to boiling over medium heat. Cover, reduce heat, and simmer just until chicken is tender (40 to 45 minutes). Remove chicken from broth, reserving broth. (Strain, reserving ¾ cup for sauce, and freeze remainder for soups or sauces.) When chicken is cool enough to handle, remove and discard bones and skin. Dice chicken into bite-size pieces. Makes 3 to 3½ cups.

MAKING AND FILLING CRÊPES

Preparing crêpe batter at least an hour ahead seems to make it smoother. Whirl it together the night before, if you wish.

Tilting and swirling the hot pan as you add batter, use just enough to cover the bottom with a thin layer.

Turn crêpes when the surface looks dry and underside is golden-brown. Use a small spatula to loosen the crêpe; turn with spatula or your fingers. Stack as they are completed.

Finished crêpes can be filled as follows; (left) place filling in center, and fold in each edge to make a square with a little filling exposed in center; for rolled crêpes, place filling in a line near edge closest to you, then roll up.

Crêpes for blintzes (left) are browned on one side only. Place filling in center of browned side, then fold in edges envelope-style. Sprinkle filling for a dessert crêpe (right) over half; fold in half lengthwise, then fold in half again to make quarters.

MEXICAN CHICKEN AND CHILE CREPES

Derived from creamy Mexican *enchiladas suizas*, this dish is made with crêpes containing just enough yellow cornmeal to give them a slight crunch.

- **3- to 3½-pound chicken, cut up**
- **2 large tomatoes, peeled and chopped**
- **½ cup water**
- **1 medium onion, finely chopped**
- **1 clove garlic, minced or pressed**
- **1 teaspoon salt**
- **¼ teaspoon *each* ground cumin and coriander**
- **1 cup whipping cream**
- **1 can (4 oz) whole green chilies, seeded and chopped**
- **Cornmeal Crêpes (recipe follows)**
- **2 cups (½ lb) shredded Monterey jack cheese**
- **½ cup sour cream, mixed until smooth with 2 tablespoons half-and-half (light cream)**
- **¼ cup sliced ripe olives**
- **3 green onions, thinly sliced (use part of tops)**

1. Place chicken pieces in a single layer in a large frying pan. Add tomatoes, water, onion, garlic, salt, cumin, and coriander. Bring to boiling over medium heat, cover, reduce heat, and simmer until chicken is very tender (about 1½ hours).

2. Remove chicken pieces from cooking liquid. When cool enough to handle, remove and discard bones and skin. Shred chicken into bite-size pieces.

3. Bring cooking liquid to boiling and boil, stirring occasionally, until sauce is thickened and reduced to about 1½ cups. Add cream, then boil again until reduced to about 2 cups. Blend in green chilies. Spread half the sauce in a shallow buttered baking dish about 9 by 13 inches.

4. Place an equal portion of chicken at end of each crêpe. Roll each crêpe and place side by side in sauce in baking dish. Spoon remaining sauce over crêpes. Sprinkle evenly with cheese. (If made ahead, cover and refrigerate.)

5. Bake, uncovered, in a 375°F oven for 20 to 30 minutes, until filling is heated through and cheese melts and browns lightly. Spoon sour cream mixture down centers of crêpes. Sprinkle with olives and green onions.

Makes 8 servings.

Cornmeal Crêpes: In blender or food processor combine ¾ cup all-purpose flour, ¼ cup yellow cornmeal, ¾ cup water, ⅔ cup milk, 3 eggs, 2 tablespoons salad oil, and ¼ teaspoon salt. Whirl or process until batter is smooth, stopping motor once or twice to stir flour down from sides of container. Cover and refrigerate batter for at least 1 hour. Blend batter well before making crêpes. Then make crêpes, using an oiled 6- to 7-inch pan. Stack as crêpes are completed. Makes 16 to 20 crêpes.

MOUSSAKA-STYLE LAMB CRÊPES

Moussaka is a Greek dish combining layers of lamb and eggplant with a custardy topping. In this variation, whole wheat crêpes replace the eggplant.

- **1½ pounds ground lamb, crumbled**
- **1 tablespoon olive oil**
- **2 medium onions, finely chopped**
- **1 clove garlic, minced or pressed (optional)**
- **¾ teaspoon ground cinnamon**
- **1 teaspoon salt**
- **⅛ teaspoon *each* ground nutmeg and white pepper**
- **¼ teaspoon dried oregano**
- **⅓ cup chopped fresh parsley**
- **1 can (8 oz) tomato sauce**
- **⅔ cup grated Parmesan cheese**
- **Whole Wheat Crêpes (recipe follows)**
- **Custard Sauce (recipe follows)**

1. Cook lamb in heated oil in a large frying pan over moderately high heat, stirring until browned. If necessary, spoon off excess fat. Mix in onions and cook, stirring occasionally, until onion is tender. Mix in garlic (if used), cinnamon, salt, nutmeg, pepper, oregano, parsley, and tomato sauce. Bring to boiling, cover, reduce heat, and simmer for 15 minutes.

2. Remove meat mixture from heat and stir in ⅓ cup of the Parmesan cheese.

3. Place an equal portion of filling at end of each crêpe. Roll each crêpe and place side by side in a shallow buttered baking dish about 9 by 13 inches.

4. Pour sauce evenly over crêpes. Sprinkle evenly with remaining ⅓ cup cheese. (If made ahead, cover and refrigerate.)

5. Bake, uncovered, in a 350°F oven until top browns lightly (45 minutes to 1 hour).

Makes 8 servings.

Whole Wheat Crêpes: In blender or food processor combine ¾ cup all-purpose flour, ¼ cup whole wheat flour, ¾ cup water, ⅔ cup milk, 3 eggs, 2 tablespoons olive oil or salad oil, and ¼ teaspoon salt. Whirl or process until batter is smooth, stopping motor once or twice to stir flour down from sides of container. Cover and refrigerate batter for at least 1 hour. Blend batter well before making crêpes. Then make crêpes, using an oiled 6- to 7-inch pan. Stack as crêpes are completed. Makes 16 to 20 crêpes.

Custard Sauce: Melt 2 tablespoons butter or margarine in a heavy, medium-size saucepan over moderate heat; stir in 2 tablespoons all-purpose flour, ½ teaspoon salt, and a dash *each* ground nutmeg and white pepper. Remove from heat and gradually stir in 2 cups milk. Cook, stirring, until thickened and boiling. In a medium bowl beat 2 eggs and 1 egg yolk. Mix in a little of the hot sauce. Off heat, blend egg mixture gradually into remaining sauce, over low heat. (Do not boil.)

TRUFFLED HAM AND CHEESE CRÊPES

It isn't absolutely necessary to include the costly truffle in these baked crêpes, but it is an elegant and impressive addition. A full-bodied dry rosé wine or a *blanc de noir* such as a "white" Zinfandel or blanc de Pinot Noir pairs well with the crêpes.

- **¼ cup finely chopped shallots *or* mild onion**
- **2 tablespoons butter**
- **1 egg**
- **¼ cup soft bread crumbs**
- **3 cups ground cooked smoked ham**
- **2 cups (½ lb) shredded Gruyère *or* Swiss cheese**
- **1 or 2 black truffles (optional)**
- **16 Basic Crêpes, 6 to 7 inches in diameter (see page 63)**
- **Wine-Cream Sauce (recipe follows)**

1. Cook shallots in butter in a small frying pan until soft and lightly browned; remove from heat.

2. In a medium bowl beat egg lightly; blend in bread crumbs and shallot mixture. Then add ham and 1 cup of the cheese. Slice truffles, if used, very thinly; reserve half the slices for topping. Sliver remaining slices and add to ham mixture. If using canned truffles, add any liquid to filling.

3. Place an equal portion of filling at end of each crêpe. Roll each crêpe and place side by side in a shallow buttered baking dish about 9 by 13 inches.

4. Pour sauce evenly over crêpes. Scatter remaining truffle slices over sauce. Sprinkle evenly with remaining 1 cup cheese. (If made ahead, cover and refrigerate.)

5. Bake, uncovered, in a 400°F oven until crêpes are heated through and lightly browned (25 to 30 minutes; about 35 minutes if refrigerated).

Makes 8 servings.

Wine-Cream Sauce: Melt 2 tablespoons butter or margarine in a medium-size, heavy saucepan. Stir in 2 tablespoons all-purpose flour and cook until bubbly. Mix in ¼ teaspoon *each* salt and dry mustard and a pinch of cayenne pepper. Remove from heat and gradually blend in 1½ cups half-and-half (light cream), then ¼ cup dry white wine. Return to heat and cook, stirring constantly, until thickened and bubbling. In a small bowl beat 1 egg yolk; gradually blend in a little of the hot sauce. Stir into remaining sauce off heat; return to low heat. Cook and stir until thick. (Do not boil.) Mix in ¼ cup grated Parmesan cheese. Makes about 2 cups.

SAVORY TURKEY CRÊPES

Somewhat reminiscent of cannelloni, these crêpes are stuffed with *uncooked* ground turkey. Therefore, they require a longer baking time than other filled crêpes that need only to be heated through. Accompany the dish with a green salad or a cooked green vegetable and a light red wine such as a young Beaujolais or a Gamay from the Loire Valley of France.

  1 **medium onion, finely chopped**
 ¼ **cup butter or margarine**
  1 **egg**
 ½ **cup each sour cream and soft bread crumbs**
  1 **teaspoon each salt and Dijon mustard**
 ⅛ **teaspoon each ground nutmeg, dried sage leaves, and white pepper**
  2 **pounds ground turkey**
16 **Basic Crêpes, 6 to 7 inches in diameter (see page 63)**
  2 **tablespoons flour**
     Pinch cayenne pepper
  1 **cup milk**
 ½ **cup canned tomato sauce**
  2 **tablespoons each dry vermouth and chopped fresh parsley**
1½ **cups shredded Gruyère or Swiss cheese**

1. Cook onion until soft and lightly browned in 2 tablespoons of the butter. In a large bowl beat egg with sour cream. Mix in bread crumbs, salt, mustard, nutmeg, sage, and pepper. Then lightly mix in turkey and cooked onions.

2. Fill crêpes with turkey mixture. Roll crêpes up and place side by side in a buttered baking dish about 9 by 13 inches.

3. For sauce, melt remaining 2 tablespoons butter in a medium saucepan. Stir in flour and cayenne; cook until bubbling. Remove from heat and gradually mix in milk, then tomato sauce (adding it about 2 tablespoons at a time). Cook, stirring, until thickened and bubbling. Remove from heat and mix in vermouth and parsley.

4. Pour tomato sauce evenly over crêpes; sprinkle with shredded cheese. (If made ahead, cover and refrigerate.)

5. Bake, uncovered, in a 375°F oven until turkey filling is cooked through and cheese browns lightly (1 to 1¼ hours).

Makes 6 to 8 servings.

ASPARAGUS AND MUSHROOM CRÊPES

Here is a tantalizing way to make a small amount of fresh asparagus serve at least 6 people — combine it with mushrooms and a cheese sauce in rolled crêpes.

  6 **tablespoons butter or margarine**
  3 **cups cut asparagus (diagonal ½-inch lengths)**
  4 **green onions, thinly sliced**
 ½ **pound mushrooms, sliced**
  1 **teaspoon each lemon juice and salt**
 ¼ **teaspoon dried tarragon**
     Dash white pepper
  2 **cups (½ lb) shredded Gruyère or Swiss cheese**
16 **Basic Crêpes, 6 to 7 inches in diameter (see page 63)**
  3 **tablespoons all-purpose flour**
  1 **teaspoon Dijon mustard**
     Dash cayenne pepper
1½ **cups half-and-half (light cream)**
 ¼ **cup dry white wine**
 ⅓ **cup grated Parmesan cheese**

1. In 3 tablespoons of the butter in a large frying pan over medium-high heat, cook and stir asparagus, green onions, and mushrooms until mushrooms brown lightly and any liquid is gone. Mix in lemon juice, ½ teaspoon of the salt, tarragon, and pepper. Remove from heat and mix in ½ cup of the Gruyère cheese.

2. Fill crêpes, dividing vegetable mixture evenly, and roll them up. Place side by side in a shallow buttered baking dish about 9 by 13 inches.

3. For sauce, melt remaining 3 tablespoons butter in a 2-quart saucepan, then stir in flour and cook until bubbly. Add remaining ½ teaspoon salt, mustard, and cayenne. Remove from heat and gradually blend in half-and-half, then wine. Return to heat and cook, stirring constantly, until thick. Stir in ½ cup more Gruyère cheese until melted.

4. Pour sauce over crêpes. Sprinkle evenly with remaining 1 cup Gruyère cheese and Parmesan cheese. (If made ahead, cover and refrigerate.)

5. Bake, uncovered, in a 400°F oven until crêpes are heated through and lightly browned (30 to 35 minutes; about 45 minutes if refrigerated).

Makes 6 to 8 servings.

An appetizing variety of fresh foods come together tastefully in Asparagus-Mushroom Crêpes.

BRETON-STYLE SAUSAGE AND SPINACH CREPES

The typical crêpes of Brittany are almost cartwheel size—as large as 12 to 15 inches in diameter. They are made on a slightly rimmed griddle of that size; unless you have traveled and shopped in Brittany, you may find the authentic article hard to obtain. For this recipe, you can make the giant crêpes using a pancake griddle (as long as it has a bit of a rim, to contain the fluid batter) or a shallow frying pan.

These crêpes are also put together differently from the preceding ones. You place a hot crêpe flat on a big plate, add the filling in the center, then fold in the four sides of the crêpe toward the center to make a plump square. French cider would be the beverage of choice in a true *crêperie*.

- 8 **Buckwheat Crêpes (recipe at right)**
- 1 **pound Polish sausage *or* other smoked garlic sausage Water**
- 1 **medium onion, finely chopped**
- ¼ **cup butter or margarine**
- 2 **packages (10 oz *each*) frozen chopped spinach, thawed and well drained**
- 1 **teaspoon flour**
- ½ **cup whipping cream**
- ¾ **teaspoon salt**
- ⅛ **teaspoon *each* ground nutmeg and white pepper**

1. Prepare batter for crêpes and let stand as directed. Make 10- to 12-inch crêpes using a large Breton crêpe pan or a pancake griddle, stacking them as each crêpe is completed. If made ahead, place in a buttered shallow pan, cover lightly with foil, and reheat in a 250°F oven until crêpes are warmed through (about 15 minutes).

2. Pierce sausages in several places with a fork. Place in a deep frying pan, pour on water to cover, and bring slowly to just under the boiling point; cover, reduce heat, and simmer very slowly for 20 minutes.

3. In a large frying pan cook onion in 2 tablespoons of the butter over medium heat until soft. Mix in spinach, flour, cream, salt, nutmeg, and white pepper. Cook, stirring often, until mixture is thick and bubbling.

4. Drain sausages and slice on the diagonal about ¼ inch thick. Cook in remaining 2 tablespoons butter in a large frying pan over moderately high heat, turning often, until sausage slices are lightly browned.

5. To assemble, place a warm crêpe on a warm plate, and spoon a dollop of spinach mixture in center. Add several browned sausage slices. Fold in edges of crêpe toward center to make a square.

Makes 8 servings.

A dessert of flaming orange crêpes caps an all-crêpe brunch menu that begins with oversized Breton buckwheat crêpes filled with sausage and spinach.

BRETON SEAFOOD CREPES

Filled with flakes of steamed fish and tiny shrimp, these buckwheat-flavored crêpes have a subtle cheese sauce.

- 1 **pound rock cod *or* sea bass fillets**
- 3 **green onions, thinly sliced (use part of tops)**
- 2 **cups (½ lb) shredded Gruyère *or* Swiss cheese**
- ½ **pound tiny peeled, cooked shrimp Buckwheat Crêpes (recipe follows)**
- 2 **tablespoons *each* butter or margarine and all-purpose flour Pinch *each* white pepper, ground nutmeg, and cayenne pepper**
- 1 **cup milk**
- ½ **cup chicken broth, homemade or canned**
- 1 **tablespoon dry vermouth**
- ½ **cup shredded Parmesan cheese**

1. Place fish fillets on a rack above about ½ inch of water in a medium frying pan. Bring water to boiling, cover, reduce heat, and steam until fish looks opaque and flakes when tested with a fork (6 to 8 minutes). Drain and cool, then remove and discard bones and skin, if any. Separate fish into flakes. (You should have about 2 cups.)

2. For filling, mix flaked fish, green onions, 1 cup of the Gruyère cheese, and about half of the shrimp. Fill crêpes, dividing seafood mixture evenly, and roll them up. Place side by side in a shallow buttered baking dish about 9 by 13 inches.

3. For sauce, melt butter in a 1½-quart saucepan over medium heat. Stir in flour, pepper, nutmeg, and cayenne; cook until bubbling. Remove from heat and gradually mix in milk and chicken broth. Cook, stirring constantly, until thickened and bubbling. Stir in remaining 1 cup Gruyère cheese until melted; fold in remaining shrimp and vermouth. Pour cheese and shrimp sauce over crêpes; sprinkle with Parmesan cheese. (If made ahead, cover and refrigerate.)

4. Bake, uncovered, in a 400°F oven until crêpes are heated through and cheese sauce is lightly browned (20 to 30 minutes).

Makes 8 servings.

Buckwheat Crêpes: In blender or food processor combine ¾ cup plus 2 tablespoons all-purpose flour, 2 tablespoons buckwheat flour, ¾ cup water, ⅔ cup milk, 3 eggs, 2 tablespoons salad oil, and ¼ teaspoon salt. Whirl or process for about 1 minute at high speed; scrape down any flour clinging to sides, then whirl or process again briefly. Cover and refrigerate batter at least 1 hour. Make 6- to 7-inch crêpes, stacking them as each crêpe is completed. Makes 16 to 20 crêpes.

ORANGE-BUTTERED DESSERT CREPES

If you would like your brunch menu to resemble that of a French *crêperie*, then the dessert that follows a crêpe main dish is a sweet crêpe. For this one the crêpes are filled with a fresh orange butter, then flamed with orange liqueur.

- 1 **cup all-purpose flour**
- 2 **tablespoons powdered sugar**
- ¾ **cup water**
- ⅔ **cup milk**
- 3 **eggs**
- 2 **tablespoons salad oil**
- ½ **teaspoon vanilla**
- ¼ **teaspoon salt Orange Butter (recipe follows)**
- ½ **cup orange-flavored liqueur (optional) *or* whipped cream to taste**

1. In blender or food processor combine flour, powdered sugar, water, milk, eggs, oil, vanilla, and salt. Whirl or process until batter is smooth, stopping motor once or twice to stir flour from sides of container. Cover and refrigerate batter for at least 1 hour.

2. Blend batter well before making crêpes, then make crêpes using a lightly oiled 6- to 7-inch pan. Stack them as each crêpe is completed. If made ahead, place in a shallow pan, cover lightly with foil, and reheat in a 250°F oven until crêpes are warmed through (about 15 minutes).

3. To serve, spoon some of the Orange Butter onto half of each crêpe, using a scant tablespoon for each; fold crêpes in quarters, and arrange, slightly overlapping, on a warm, rimmed, heatproof platter.

4. If you wish, flame the crêpes by heating liqueur in a small metal pan until *barely warm* to touch. (Liqueur will not flame if overheated.) Ignite carefully and pour, flaming, over crêpes. Lift crêpes with 2 forks until flames die out. Serve at once on warm plates. If you do not flame the crêpes, serve crêpes with whipped cream.

Makes 6 servings.

Orange Butter: In a medium bowl beat ½ cup butter or margarine (softened) until fluffy. Gradually beat in ½ cup sugar, then blend in grated rind of 1 orange. Adding about 2 teaspoons at a time, gradually beat in 3 tablespoons orange juice. (If made ahead, cover and refrigerate; let stand at room temperature at least 1 hour before serving). Makes about 1 cup.

Make blintzes ahead, including the filling and the folding, and refrigerate them. Later, brown the blintzes and serve them hot with sour cream and cherry preserves.

¾ **cup all-purpose flour**
¼ **teaspoon baking soda**
½ **teaspoon salt**
2 **tablespoons sugar**
1 **cup buttermilk**
½ **cup water**
3 **eggs**
2 **tablespoons vegetable oil**
 Cheese Filling (recipe follows)
3 **to 4 tablespoons *each* butter or margarine and vegetable oil, for frying**
 Sour cream
 Cherry preserves

1. In blender or food processor combine flour, soda, salt, sugar, buttermilk, water, eggs, and oil. Whirl or process until batter is smooth, stopping motor once or twice to stir flour from sides of container. Cover and refrigerate for at least 1 hour before using batter.

2. Make blintzes in a lightly oiled 6- to 7-inch pan as for crêpes, but brown them *on first side only* and cook until top surface is dry to touch. Stack blintzes on a paper towel to cool.

3. To fill each blintz, place a dollop (about 2 tablespoons) of Cheese Filling in center of browned side of each pancake. Fold in opposite edges about 1 inch, then fold in remaining edges to enclose filling, over-lapping in center to make a slightly rectangular-shaped "envelope." Set blintzes aside, folded side down. (If made ahead, cover and refrigerate.)

4. In a large frying pan over moderately high heat, melt 2 tablespoons of the butter with 2 tablespoons of the oil. Fry filled blintzes without crowding until golden on each side (1 to 1½ minutes on each side). Add more butter and oil to pan as needed.

5. Drain blintzes and serve on warm plates, topped with sour cream and preserves.

Makes 20 to 24 blintzes (6 to 8 servings).

Cheese Filling: In a large bowl beat 1 package (8 oz) softened cream cheese with 1 egg, 2 tablespoons powdered sugar, ½ teaspoon vanilla, and ¼ teaspoon ground cinnamon. Then beat in 1 pound (about 2 cups) pot cheese (also called farmer's cheese). Makes about 3 cups.

ALMOND DESSERT CRÊPES

Amaretto liqueur flavors the filling of these almond-sprinkled baked dessert crêpes. Serve them hot with lightly whipped cream.

18 **to 20 Dessert Crêpes (see page 67)**
⅓ **cup butter or margarine, softened**
⅓ **cup sugar**
½ **teaspoon *each* grated lemon rind and almond extract**
1 **egg**
1 **tablespoon amaretto liqueur**
¼ **cup all-purpose flour**
1 **cup ground blanched almonds (whirled in blender or food processor until powdery)**
2 **tablespoons butter or margarine**
¼ **cup sliced almonds**
 Whipped cream

1. Make Dessert Crêpes in a lightly oiled 6- to 7-inch pan. Stack them as each crêpe is completed; set aside while preparing filling.

2. In a medium bowl beat the ⅓ cup butter until fluffy. Gradually beat in sugar, then blend in lemon rind and almond extract. Beat in egg until smoothly blended. Mix in liqueur, then flour and ground almonds. Beat until well combined.

3. Place an equal portion of filling at end of each crêpe. Roll each crêpe and place side by side in a shallow buttered baking dish about 9 by 13 inches. Dot with the 2 tablespoons butter, then sprinkle with sliced almonds.

4. Bake in a 425°F oven until crêpes are hot and edges are crisp (10 to 12 minutes). Serve hot with whipped cream.

Makes 6 to 8 servings.

BUTTERMILK BLINTZES

Blintzes aren't crêpes, but you can make these thin pancakes in a crêpe pan. The difference in technique is that at first the blintzes are browned on only one side. After they have been wrapped around a distinctive cheese filling, the blintzes are then fried to brown the other side.

Making blintzes is a lengthy operation. If you make them ahead, you can cover and refrigerate the filled blintzes for up to 24 hours. Then brown them quickly and serve hot.

OVEN PANCAKES

A popover-like batter baked in a large round or square pan puffs spectacularly and forms a crisp crust. This sort of oven pancake serves several people easily and invites variations, either additions to the batter before baking or toppings afterward.

TOAD-IN-THE-HOLE

This English dish is a lot like Yorkshire pudding, but rather than being served as an accompaniment to roast beef, it is a main dish studded with chunks of sausage. For brunch, add mustard pickles or a green salad with a mustard-flavored vinaigrette dressing and toasted country bread.

        2   **eggs**
        ¾   **cup milk**
        ¼   **cup water**
        1   **cup all-purpose flour**
        ¼   **teaspoon salt**
        1   **pound Italian sausages**
        ¼   **cup butter or margarine**

1. In blender or food processor combine eggs, milk, water, flour, and salt; whirl or process, stopping motor to scrape down sides of container once or twice. Refrigerate batter for 1 hour or longer.

2. Pierce each sausage in several places with a fork. Brown slowly on all sides over medium heat in a large frying pan for 8 to 10 minutes. Reserve drippings. Cut sausages into 1½-inch chunks.

3. Place butter in a 9-inch-square baking pan, 10-inch quiche dish, or 10-inch pie pan. Heat in a 375°F oven until butter melts (5 to 8 minutes). Then add reserved sausage drippings and chunks of sausage. Pour in batter.

4. Bake in 375°F oven until pancake is puffy and well browned (30 to 35 minutes). Cut into squares or wedges and serve immediately.

Makes 4 to 6 servings.

HONEYED OVEN PANCAKE

Summer fruits complement this honey-sweetened oven pancake. Try it with honey-drizzled sliced peaches or nectarines, the Peaches and Blueberries with Cream on page 21 (if you use the cream, whip it until stiff), or sliced strawberries with sour cream and brown sugar.

        3   **tablespoons butter or margarine**
        3   **eggs**
        3   **tablespoons honey**
        ¼   **teaspoon salt**
      1¾   **cups milk**
        ¾   **cup all-purpose flour**
            Fresh fruit topping, as suggested above

1. Place butter in a 10-inch pie pan, 10-inch quiche dish, or 10-inch frying pan with heatproof handle. Place pan in 425°F oven as it preheats; when butter is melted, remove pan from oven. (Do not let butter burn.)

2. While butter is melting, beat eggs with honey, salt, and milk. Then beat in flour until mixture is smooth. Pour batter into melted butter in hot pan.

3. Bake in 425°F oven until pancake is browned, edges are puffed, and a knife inserted in center comes out clean (20 to 25 minutes). Cut in wedges and serve immediately, adding fruit topping at the table.

Makes 3 to 4 servings.

FRENCH TOAST

If you were served French toast in France, it would be called pain perdu *or "lost bread" — yesterday's bread rescued from inedibility by dipping it in a mixture of egg and milk, then browning in butter. It is a fine way of making a breakfast specialty with a few ingredients that are usually at hand.*

JAM-FILLED FRENCH TOAST

Sourdough bread is a fine flavor foil for the luscious center of preserves in each thick slice of this French toast. Serve more of the same preserves or jam on the side if you wish.

        8   **slices (each 1½ in. thick) day-old sourdough French bread**
        ½   **cup Strawberry-Rhubarb Preserves (see page 94) or other favorite fruit preserves, jam, or marmalade**
        2   **eggs**
        1   **tablespoon granulated sugar**
        ¾   **cup milk**
        ½   **teaspoon vanilla**
        ⅛   **teaspoon ground cinnamon**
        2   **tablespoons butter or margarine**
        1   **tablespoon salad oil**
            Powdered sugar

1. Cutting from bottom of each slice through center almost to top, slash a pocket in each piece of bread. Squeeze bread slice lightly to open pocket and fill each pocket with about 1 tablespoon of the preserves.

2. In a shallow bowl beat eggs with granulated sugar, milk, vanilla, and cinnamon. Dip each filled bread slice in egg mixture to coat well.

3. In a large, shallow frying pan melt 1 tablespoon of the butter with oil over medium heat until mixture is foamy. Add bread slices, 4 at a time, and cook until well browned and crisp on each side, turning once and adding remaining 1 tablespoon butter as needed.

4. Serve French toast hot, sprinkled with powdered sugar.

Makes 4 servings.

Toad-in-the-Hole is a heartier sort of oven pancake, reminiscent of Yorkshire pudding. Studded with sausage chunks, it is good with a green salad and a country-style bread.

BREAKFAST IN BED

**French Toast with Strawberries
Vanilla Sugar   Sour Cream
Sautéed Canadian-Style Bacon
Breakfast Tea**

Treat someone to a breakfast in bed of cinnamon-spiced French toast garlanded by sliced fresh strawberries sweetened with fragrant vanilla sugar.

Thinly sliced Canadian-style bacon needs only a brief turning in heated butter in another pan while the French toast is browning and the tea steeps.

FRENCH TOAST WITH STRAWBERRIES

    2 cups strawberries
      Vanilla Sugar (see page 22)
    3 eggs
    2 teaspoons sugar
    ¼ teaspoon ground cinnamon
    ½ cup half-and-half (light cream)
    8 slices French bread
    ¼ to ½ cup butter or margarine
      Sour cream

1. Remove and discard hulls from berries; slice and sweeten to taste with some of the Vanilla Sugar. Set aside while preparing French toast.

2. Beat eggs with sugar, cinnamon, and half-and-half in a shallow dish. Dip bread slices in egg mixture to coat well.

3. Brown bread slices on both sides in heated butter in a large frying pan over medium heat, starting with 2 tablespoons butter and adding more as needed. Keep French toast warm in a 250°F oven until all is ready.

4. Serve French toast with strawberries spooned over and a dollop of sour cream on each piece. Serve additional Vanilla Sugar to taste.

Makes 4 servings.

MONTE CRISTO SANDWICH

A French-toasted ham, cheese, and turkey sandwich makes a stylish brunch dish. The traditional finish for this hot sandwich is a dusting of powdered sugar and a dollop of currant jelly, but you can omit them if you prefer less sweetness.

    8 slices white bread, crusts
      trimmed
    8 thin slices (about 4 oz) Swiss
      cheese, cut to fit bread
    4 slices (3 oz) baked ham
    4 slices (3 oz) roast turkey breast
    2 eggs
    ¼ cup half-and-half (light cream)
      Pinch *each* ground nutmeg and
      white pepper
    2 tablespoons butter or
      margarine
      Powdered sugar and red
      currant jelly (optional)

1. To make sandwiches, place on each of 4 slices of the bread, in order: a slice *each* of Swiss cheese, ham, turkey, then another slice of Swiss cheese. Complete each sandwich with another slice of bread. Cut sandwiches in halves.

2. Beat eggs in a shallow bowl with half-and-half, nutmeg, and white pepper. Dip sandwiches in egg mixture to coat well on both sides.

3. Brown lightly on both sides in butter in a large frying pan over medium heat, turning sandwiches once. Place sandwiches on a baking sheet and bake in a 400°F oven until cheese melts (3 to 5 minutes).

4. If you wish, sprinkle lightly with powdered sugar and accompany with currant jelly. Serve hot to eat with knives and forks.

Makes 4 sandwiches.

WAFFLES

The iron in which waffles are baked — and which gives them their distinctive gridlike pattern — may take a round, square, or rectangular shape. Some irons are electric; others are designed for use on top of the range. In any case, the grids of a waffle iron — like a crêpe pan or a pancake griddle — should be seasoned well and then never washed. Season the grids before first use as you would an omelet or crêpe pan (see page 6), or follow the manufacturer's directions for seasoning a waffle iron with a nonstick coating. If you don't use your waffle iron often, brush the grids lightly with salad oil before heating the iron.

SESAME WAFFLES

Sesame seeds add a nutlike flavor to these crisp waffles, to serve with a favorite syrup or honey.

    1 cup all-purpose flour
    1½ teaspoons baking powder
    ⅛ teaspoon salt
    1 tablespoon sesame seeds
    2 eggs, separated
    ¾ cup milk
    ½ teaspoon vanilla
    ¼ cup butter or margarine, melted
      and cooled
      Butter or margarine and maple
      syrup

1. Stir together flour, baking powder, salt, and sesame seeds. Beat egg yolks with milk in a large bowl. Blend in vanilla and melted butter. Then add flour mixture and stir just until combined.

2. Beat egg whites until stiff but not dry. Fold into batter.

3. Spoon batter into center of heated waffle iron, using about a fourth of the batter for each waffle. Bake about 5 minutes or until steaming stops. Remove waffles carefully and serve at once with butter and syrup.

Makes four 7-inch waffles (4 servings).

SCANDINAVIAN HEART-SHAPED WAFFLES

These unusual sour cream waffles are made in the charming waffle iron shown on page 61. You might make them to serve as part of a Scandinavian breakfast buffet with herring, sliced cold meats, cheeses, crisp flatbread, and lots of coffee. The waffles can be made ahead and reheated in a low oven. They're easiest to eat as a finger food, like cookies.

    ¾ cup all-purpose flour
    2 teaspoons baking powder
    2 eggs, separated
    1¼ cups sour cream
    1 tablespoon salad oil
      Powdered sugar and
      lingonberry *or* tart cherry
      preserves

1. Stir together flour and baking powder. Beat egg yolks with sour cream in a large bowl. Blend in oil. Then add flour mixture and stir just until combined.

2. Beat egg whites until stiff but not dry. Fold into batter.

3. Spoon a generous tablespoon of batter into each section of heated heart-shaped waffle iron. Bake until golden brown (about 2 minutes on first side and 3 minutes on the second).

4. Serve hot sprinkled with powdered sugar and with a dollop of preserves.

Makes 5 waffles (4 to 6 servings).

BELGIAN WAFFLES WITH BLUEBERRY SAUCE

Made from a yeast batter, these waffles with their fresh berry sauce are a summer treat. A special waffle iron, imported from France, gives the deep, rectangular shape (see page 61).

- **1 package active dry yeast**
- **¼ cup warm water**
- **2 cups all-purpose flour**
- **¼ cup sugar**
- **¼ teaspoon salt**
- **¼ cup butter or margarine, melted and cooled**
- **2 tablespoons salad oil**
- **1½ cups water**
- **½ teaspoon vanilla**
- **2 eggs, separated**
  Blueberry Sauce (recipe follows)
  Whipped cream (optional)

1. Sprinkle yeast over the ¼ cup warm water in a small bowl; let stand about 5 minutes to soften. In a large bowl mix flour, sugar, and salt. Beat in butter, oil, the 1½ cups water, and vanilla until smooth. Then beat in egg yolks and yeast mixture.

2. Beat egg whites until they form soft peaks; fold gently into batter. Cover and refrigerate for several hours or overnight; stir down batter.

3. Place a seasoned 6- by 7½-inch Belgian waffle iron directly over medium heat, turning it over occasionally, until a few drops of water dance on the grids. Spoon about ½ cup batter into the iron, spreading it to just cover grids.

4. Close the iron and turn it occasionally until waffle is well browned (4 to 5 minutes in all). Transfer waffles to a wire rack unless served immediately.

5. If made ahead, cool waffles, wrap in foil, and freeze. Then reheat, uncovered, in a single layer on baking sheets in a 325°F oven until hot and crisp (about 10 minutes).

6. Serve hot, with hot Blueberry Sauce poured over. Add whipped cream if you wish.

Makes 9 waffles (6 to 8 servings).

Blueberry Sauce: Combine ⅓ cup butter or margarine, ⅔ cup sugar, and 3 tablespoons light corn syrup in a medium saucepan. Place over medium heat and cook, stirring, until mixture boils. Mix in ¼ cup water and bring again to boiling; boil for 2 minutes. Add 2 teaspoons grated lemon rind, ¼ teaspoon ground nutmeg, and 1½ cups fresh or frozen unsweetened blueberries. Cook, stirring, until mixture boils. Serve hot. Makes about 1¾ cups.

GRILLED CHEESE-AND-TOMATO SANDWICHES

They aren't waffles, but the intriguing *croque monsieur* iron—it gives a shell-like imprint—used to grill these sandwiches on top of the range so resembles a Belgian waffle iron that the recipe is included here. Those who like something more rib-sticking than toast and jelly in the morning will find these hot sandwiches satisfying.

- **4 slices whole wheat, rye, or egg bread**
  Mustard (optional)
- **6 slices (3 oz) Swiss or Cheddar cheese, cut to fit bread**
- **2 thin slices firm-ripe tomato**
  Butter or margarine

1. Spread 2 of the bread slices lightly with mustard of your choice. (Try coarsely ground or tarragon-flavored Dijon mustard.) Cover each with half of the cheese and a tomato slice. Place remaining bread slices over tomatoes to complete sandwiches.

2. Spread tops of sandwiches generously with butter. Place, buttered side down, in seasoned croque monsieur toasting iron or on greased griddle. Spread other side of sandwiches generously with butter. If using a croque monsieur iron, close it and hook the latch on the handle; if any bread extends beyond edges, trim and discard it.

3. Place iron or griddle over medium heat and cook sandwiches until well browned on both sides, turning once (4 to 5 minutes on first side, then 2 to 3 minutes on second). Serve at once.

Makes 2 sandwiches.

PUFFY CORN FRITTERS

Here is another dish that isn't a pancake, crêpe, or waffle. The reason these simple corn fritters appear with these foods is that they share an affinity to maple syrup. You might also serve them, without the syrup, as a vegetable accompaniment to breakfast meats.

- **⅓ cup all-purpose flour**
- **½ teaspoon salt**
  Pinch ground coriander
- **2 eggs, separated**
- **1 package (10 oz) frozen whole-kernel corn, thawed**
  Salad oil for frying
  Syrup (optional)

1. Stir together flour, salt, and coriander. In a large bowl beat egg yolks slightly. Mix in corn. Add flour mixture, mixing until blended.

2. Beat egg whites until stiff but not dry. Fold into corn mixture.

3. Pour oil into a deep, heavy frying pan to a depth of about ¼ inch. Heat over medium heat until a bit of the corn mixture sizzles when dropped into the oil. Drop corn mixture by rounded tablespoons into oil. Cook fritters until golden brown on each side, turning once (3 to 4 minutes in all). Drain well.

4. Serve fritters hot with syrup or as an accompaniment to other breakfast dishes.

Makes 20 fritters (4 to 6 servings).

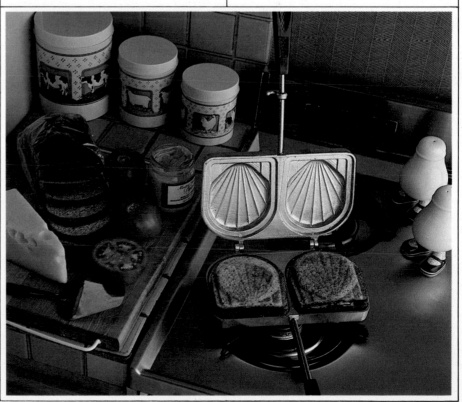

A croque monsieur iron (see page 61) makes grilled breakfast sandwiches that are as handsome as they are satisfying.

Quiche is the classic breakfast pie. And Chicken Pot Pie is wonderful for brunch. So is a celebrational fresh fruit tart late on a weekend morn.

PIE FOR BREAKFAST

If you like pie, probably you can't resist a flaky wedge of it for breakfast—or for brunch, anyway. The possibilities for enclosing morning foods in crusts are vast: from creamy quiches puffed with eggs, cheese, vegetables, or bits of ham, through shattery filo dough-wrapped pastries and loaves of stuffed brioche, to generous fruit tarts that bring a full-scale brunch to a memorable conclusion.

QUICHES

The pastries involved in breakfast pies take many forms. For a quiche, use an egg-rich flaky pastry, shortened with a combination of butter and lard. A mixture of all-purpose flour and a touch of whole wheat or rye flour or cornmeal will give a quiche crust a flavor and texture boost.

EGG PASTRY FOR QUICHE

- 1 ¼ **cups all-purpose flour**
- ¼ **teaspoon salt**
- ¼ **cup butter or margarine**
- 2 **tablespoons lard**
- 1 **egg, slightly beaten**

1. In a medium bowl mix flour and salt. Cut in butter and lard until mixture is crumbly.

2. Gradually add egg to flour mixture, stirring until it is evenly moistened and begins to cling together. Shape into a flattened ball.

3. Roll out on a floured board or pastry cloth to about a 13-inch circle. Fit pastry into a 10-inch quiche dish. Trim edge to about a ½-inch overhang, then fold pastry under, even with top of dish.

4. Fill and bake as directed in following recipes.

LEEK QUICHE

Briefly cooked leeks give this meatless quiche a French accent. To complete a brunch menu, add sliced baked ham and a simple leafy lettuce salad.

- 3 **large leeks**
- 2 **tablespoons butter or margarine**
  Unbaked Egg Pastry (recipe at left)
- 1 ¼ **cups shredded Gruyère *or* Swiss cheese**
- 3 **eggs**
- 1 **cup half-and-half (light cream)**
- 1 **teaspoon Dijon mustard**
- ½ **teaspoon salt**
  Pinch *each* white pepper and ground nutmeg

1. Cut off root ends of leeks; remove coarse outer leaves. Cut off upper parts of green tops, leaving about 10-inch-long leeks. Split lengthwise, from stem ends, cutting to within about 1 inch of root ends. Soak in cold water to cover for several minutes; then separate leaves under running water to rinse away any clinging grit; drain well. Slice about ⅛ inch thick.

2. In a large frying pan melt butter over medium heat. Add sliced leeks; cook, stirring often, until leeks are limp and bright green (6 to 8 minutes). Distribute leeks evenly in pastry shell. Sprinkle with 1 cup of the cheese.

3. Beat eggs with half-and-half, mustard, salt, pepper, and nutmeg; pour over cheese.

4. Bake quiche in a 450°F oven for 10 minutes; reduce heat to 350°F and continue baking for 15 minutes longer. Sprinkle quiche evenly with remaining ¼ cup cheese, then bake for 5 to 10 minutes more, until crust is nicely browned and filling is just set in center.

5. Let stand about 3 minutes before cutting in wedges to serve.

Makes 6 servings.

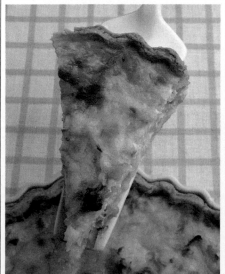

An egg and butter-rich pastry (left) is the foundation for the varied and delicious quiches in this chapter. At right is a steaming wedge of savory Leek Quiche.

Asparagus spears radiate from the center of a spring quiche in which tiny shrimp are hidden.

crab or shrimp, pepper, and parsley. Distribute shellfish mixture evenly in pastry shell. Sprinkle with cheese, then arrange asparagus spears, like spokes, over it.

3. Beat eggs with half-and-half, salt, mustard, and paprika; pour over asparagus.

4. Bake quiche in a 450°F oven for 10 minutes; reduce heat to 350°F and continue baking for 20 to 25 minutes longer, until crust is well browned and filling is set in center.

5. Let stand about 3 minutes before cutting in wedges to serve.

Makes 6 to 8 servings.

FRESH SALMON QUICHE

Fresh salmon, lightly steamed, makes this splendid quiche a good choice for a spring or summer brunch. You might accompany it with a green salad containing sliced papaya and mixed with a lime juice and oil dressing.

- ½ **pound salmon fillet**
  Water
- 4 **green onions, thinly sliced**
- 2 **tablespoons butter or margarine**
- ½ **teaspoon dried dillweed**
  Unbaked Egg Pastry (see page 73)
- 1 **cup shredded Swiss cheese**
- 3 **eggs**
- 1 **cup half-and-half (light cream)**
- ¾ **teaspoon salt**
- ½ **teaspoon dry mustard**
  Pinch white pepper

1. Place salmon on a rack over about ½ inch of water in a medium frying pan. Bring water to boiling, cover, reduce heat, and steam until salmon flakes when tested with a fork (6 to 8 minutes). Remove and discard skin and flake salmon gently.

2. Cook onions in butter in a medium frying pan over moderate heat until limp and bright green (about 3 minutes). Remove from heat; mix in salmon and dillweed. Distribute salmon mixture evenly in pastry shell. Sprinkle with cheese.

3. Beat eggs with half-and-half, salt, mustard, and pepper; pour over cheese.

4. Bake quiche in a 450°F oven for 10 minutes; reduce heat to 350°F and continue baking for 20 to 25 minutes longer, until crust is nicely browned and filling is just set in center.

5. Let stand about 3 minutes before cutting in wedges to serve.

Makes 6 servings.

BLUE CHEESE QUICHE

Any blue-veined cheese will give this creamy quiche a wonderfully piquant flavor, but for a real treat use true French Roquefort.

- ½ **cup crumbled blue-veined cheese**
- 1 **cup shredded Swiss cheese**
  Unbaked Egg Pastry (see page 73)
- 2 **shallots, finely chopped** *or* ¼ **cup finely chopped mild onion**
- 2 **tablespoons butter or margarine**
- 4 **eggs**
- 1 **cup half-and-half (light cream)**
- 1 **teaspoon Dijon mustard**
- ½ **teaspoon salt**
- ¼ **teaspoon** *each* **paprika and ground nutmeg**
  Pinch white pepper

1. Distribute cheeses evenly in pastry shell. Cook shallots in butter in a small frying pan over medium heat until soft and golden; sprinkle mixture over cheeses.

2. Beat eggs with half-and-half, mustard, salt, paprika, nutmeg, and pepper; pour over cheese.

3. Bake quiche in a 450°F oven for 10 minutes; reduce heat to 350°F and continue baking for 20 to 25 minutes longer, until quiche is nicely browned and just set in center.

4. Let stand about 3 minutes before cutting in wedges to serve.

Makes 6 servings.

ASPARAGUS AND SEAFOOD QUICHE

Either crab or tiny shrimp complement the spokes of fresh asparagus in this handsome quiche. For brunch serve a Chardonnay or Fumé Blanc wine with the pie.

- 6 **to 8 asparagus spears (about ¾ lb)**
  Salted water
- ¼ **cup finely chopped shallots** *or* **mild onion**
- 2 **tablespoons butter or margarine**
- ½ **pound cooked crab, flaked** *or* **tiny peeled, cooked shrimp**
  Pinch white pepper
- ¼ **cup chopped fresh parsley**
  Unbaked Egg Pastry (see page 73)
- 1 **cup shredded Swiss cheese**
- 4 **eggs**
- 1⅓ **cups half-and-half (light cream)**
- ½ **teaspoon salt**
- 1 **teaspoon Dijon mustard**
- ¼ **teaspoon paprika**

1. Snap off fibrous ends of asparagus spears; cook, uncovered, in a small amount of boiling salted water in a wide frying pan just until bright green and barely tender-crisp (3 to 4 minutes). Drain and reserve.

2. Cook shallots in butter until soft but not brown; remove from heat and lightly mix in

HAM AND CHEESE CUSTARD PIE

Quichelike, this creamy breakfast pie is baked in a crispy rye pastry.

- ½ **pound thinly sliced baked *or* boiled ham, cut in thin strips**
- 2 **tablespoons butter or margarine**
  Unbaked Rye Pastry (recipe follows)
- ¼ **cup grated Parmesan cheese**
- 5 **eggs**
- 1 **cup sour cream**
- ½ **teaspoon salt**
  Pinch *each* ground nutmeg and white pepper

1. Cook ham in heated butter in a large frying pan, stirring occasionally over medium heat until ham strips are lightly browned. Spoon evenly into pastry shell. Sprinkle with cheese.

2. Beat eggs well with sour cream, salt, nutmeg, and pepper. Pour over ham and cheese.

3. Bake in a 450°F oven for 10 minutes; reduce heat to 350°F and continue baking for 20 to 25 minutes, until crust is nicely browned and filling is just set in center.

4. Let stand about 3 minutes before cutting in wedges to serve.

Makes 6 servings.

Rye Pastry: In a large bowl mix 1 cup all-purpose flour, ¼ cup rye flour, and ¼ teaspoon salt. Cut in ¼ cup firm butter or margarine and 2 tablespoons lard or soft shortening until mixture forms coarse crumbs. Beat 1 egg yolk with 2 tablespoons cold water; gradually mix into flour mixture, stirring with a fork until pastry clings together. Shape with your hands into a smooth ball. Roll out on a floured board or pastry cloth to a circle. Fit pastry into a 9-inch pie pan; trim and flute edge.

CHICKEN POT PIE

Made in every respect from scratch, this traditional chicken pie with a cornmeal-accented top crust is a bit of a chore. However, it can be entirely assembled in advance, then refrigerated overnight. Bake it the morning of the brunch and dazzle everyone with its homemade flavor.

- **Simmered Chicken and Broth (recipe follows)**
- ¼ **cup butter or margarine**
- 1 **small onion, finely chopped**
- ¼ **pound mushrooms, thinly sliced**
- 2 **tablespoons all-purpose flour**
  Dash *each* white pepper and nutmeg
- ½ **cup julienne ham**
- ½ **cup thawed frozen peas**
  Cornmeal Pastry (recipe follows)

1. Prepare chicken and broth as directed.

2. In a large, heavy saucepan melt butter over medium heat. In it cook onion and mushrooms until mushrooms brown lightly. Stir in flour, pepper, and nutmeg, cooking until bubbly. Remove from heat and gradually stir in the 1½ cups reserved chicken broth. Return to heat and cook, stirring, until mixture is thickened.

3. Mix in chicken pieces, ham strips, and peas. Taste, and add salt if needed. Spread chicken mixture in a 10-inch quiche dish or a 10-inch pie plate. Place pastry over chicken mixture; trim edge so that it extends about ¾ inch beyond edge of baking dish. Fold pastry edge under, flush with edge of dish; press firmly against edge of quiche dish, or flute edge if using a pie plate. Cut slits in top for steam to escape. (If made ahead, cover and refrigerate.)

4. Beat egg white reserved from pastry with 1 teaspoon water. Brush over top of crust. Bake in a 425°F oven until pastry is well browned and filling bubbles (25 to 30 minutes).

Makes 6 servings.

Simmered Chicken and Broth: Cut 1 large frying chicken (3½ to 4 lbs) into serving pieces. In a 4- to 5-quart kettle or Dutch oven combine chicken pieces, 1 small onion (coarsely chopped), 1 medium carrot (cut in ½-inch slices), 2 sprigs parsley, ½ bay leaf, 1 stalk celery (coarsely chopped), 1 teaspoon salt, ¼ teaspoon dried thyme, and 3 cups water. Bring to boiling, reduce heat, cover, and simmer until chicken is very tender (1¼ to 1½ hours). Strain and reserve broth; measure 1½ cups of the broth for pie and freeze remainder for another use. Remove chicken from bones, discarding bones, skin, and cooked vegetables. Divide chicken into generous bite-size pieces (about 3 cups).

Cornmeal Pastry: In a large bowl mix 1 cup all-purpose flour, ¼ cup yellow cornmeal, and ¼ teaspoon salt. Cut in ¼ cup firm butter or margarine and 2 tablespoons lard or soft shortening until mixture forms coarse crumbs. Beat 1 egg yolk with 2 tablespoons cold water (reserve egg white to glaze pastry); gradually mix into flour mixture, stirring with a fork until pastry clings together. Shape with your hands into a smooth ball. Roll out on a floured board or pastry cloth to a circle about 12 inches in diameter.

A cornmeal-accented pastry cloaks the chicken, ham, mushrooms, and peas in this pot pie.

PATIO BRUNCH

Mimosas (see page 18)
Sweet Corn and Bacon Quiche
Sliced Tomatoes
Fresh Strawberry Torte
Coffee

Summertime produce —sweet corn, juicy strawberries —are featured in the two special dishes of this warm-weather brunch. As guests arrive and the quiche finishes baking, offer them Mimosas, lovely froths of Champagne and fresh orange juice, to sip.

To keep last-minute preparations to a minimum, have the unbaked cornmeal pastry shell containing corn, cheese, and bacon done ahead (covered and refrigerated), and the egg mixture ready to add just before the quiche goes into the oven.

The strawberry dessert pastry can be made several hours ahead or the evening before. Add its garnish of whipped cream and toasted almonds shortly before serving.

SWEET CORN AND BACON QUICHE

    6 slices bacon, cut crosswise in ½-
       inch strips
       Unbaked Cornmeal Pastry Shell
       (recipe follows)
    2 ears corn, kernels cut from cobs
       (1½ to 2 cups corn)
    1 cup shredded Cheddar cheese
    5 eggs
 1 ½ cups half-and-half (light cream)
    ½ teaspoon salt
       Pinch cayenne pepper

1. Cook bacon until lightly browned; drain on paper towel.

2. In pastry shell evenly distribute corn, cheese, and bacon. Beat eggs with half-and-half, salt, and cayenne. Pour egg mixture over corn, cheese, and bacon.

3. Bake quiche in a 450°F oven for 10 minutes; reduce heat to 350°F and continue baking for 20 to 25 minutes longer, until quiche is nicely browned and just set in center.

4. Let stand for about 3 minutes before cutting in wedges to serve.

Makes 6 to 8 servings.

Pie lovers take notice—this menu for a warm weather brunch on the patio presents two of them. The main course is a quiche with sweet corn, bacon, and cheese; for dessert there is a luscious fresh strawberry torte with an almond pastry.

Cornmeal Pastry Shell: In a medium bowl mix 1 cup all-purpose flour, ¼ cup yellow cornmeal, ¼ teaspoon salt, and 2 tablespoons grated Parmesan cheese. Cut in ¼ cup butter or margarine and 2 tablespoons lard until mixture is crumbly. Beat 1 egg; gradually add to flour mixture, stirring until it is evenly moistened and begins to cling together. Shape into a flattened ball. Roll out on a floured board or pastry cloth to about a 13-inch circle. Fit pastry into a 10-inch quiche dish, trimming about ½ inch above top edge. Then press edge under even with top of dish.

FRESH STRAWBERRY TORTE

       Almond Press-In Pastry (see
       page 81)
    4 cups strawberries
    1 cup granulated sugar
    2 tablespoons *each* cornstarch
       and lemon juice
    1 cup whipping cream
    2 teaspoons powdered sugar
       Dash vanilla
    2 tablespoons toasted sliced
       almonds

1. Press pastry into the bottom and halfway up the sides of a 9-inch springform pan. Using a fork, pierce sides and bottom of the pastry. Bake in a 425°F oven for 10 to 12 minutes, until lightly browned. Cool in pan on a wire rack.

2. Remove and discard hulls from berries. Place half of the berries in a medium saucepan and crush them with a fork. Mix in granulated sugar, cornstarch, and lemon juice. Cook over medium heat, stirring, until thickened and transparent (about 10 minutes). Cool until lukewarm.

3. Cut remaining berries into halves; fold them into cooked strawberry mixture. Spread filling in pastry shell and refrigerate until filling is set (1 to 2 hours). (Cover if refrigerated any longer.)

4. Remove sides of pan. Whip cream with powdered sugar and vanilla until stiff. Spread or mound over berry filling. Sprinkle with almonds. Cut in wedges to serve.

Makes 8 to 10 servings.

SAVORY FILO-WRAPPED PASTRIES

For these filo dough-wrapped pastries, use the paper-thin sheets of filo sold in 1-pound packages, refrigerated or frozen, in stores that feature Greek and other ethnic foods. A package of filo is a versatile ingredient to keep on hand in the freezer, since it can be used for a number of breakfast pastries.

BAKED BREAKFAST REUBENS

Really a cross-cultural combination, these puffy rectangular pastries enclose the popular corned beef, sauerkraut, and Swiss cheese sandwich filling in a flaky filo wrapping.

   12 sheets (about ½ lb) filo dough,
       thawed if frozen
    6 tablespoons to ½ cup
       butter or margarine, melted
   12 thin slices corned beef
       Russian Dressing (recipe
       follows)
    1 small can (8 oz) sauerkraut,
       drained
    ½ pound thinly sliced Swiss
       cheese

1. Unfold sheets of filo dough so they lie flat. Cover with plastic wrap, then a damp towel, to prevent them from drying out. Remove one sheet of filo at a time, brush half lightly with melted butter, and fold in half to make a rectangle about 9 by 12 inches. Brush again with butter.

2. At one narrow end place slice of corned beef, folded to make about a 3- by 5-inch rectangle. Top with a dollop of dressing, then sauerkraut, and finally cheese (folded to same size as corned beef). Fold in sides of filo about 1½ inches, then starting at end with filling, turn over 3 times to make an envelope-shaped packet. Place seam side down on greased baking sheets. Repeat for remaining dough and filling. (If made ahead, cover and refrigerate.) Brush lightly with remaining butter.

3. Bake in a 350°F oven until golden brown (20 to 25 minutes). Serve hot.

Makes 12 sandwiches (6 servings).

Russian Dressing: Mix ¼ cup mayonnaise, 1 tablespoon chili sauce, pinch cayenne pepper, and 2 tablespoons finely chopped stuffed olives.

Makes a scant ½ cup.

GREEK SPINACH PIE

Buttery-crisp layers of filo dough, top and bottom, make an irresistible vegetable pie known in Greece as *spanokopita*. It can be served hot, warm, or at room temperature.

If you would like to make this the centerpiece of a brunch inspired by Greek cooking, add tiny lamb chops grilled with olive oil and oregano, with lemon to squeeze over; a loaf of sesame-seeded bread; and a salad of tomatoes, cucumber, pepper strips, and ripe olives.

- 2 bunches (about ¾ lb *each*) spinach
- 1 medium onion, finely chopped
- 1 bunch (6 to 8) green onions, thinly sliced (use part of tops)
- ¼ cup olive oil
- 1 tablespoon dried dillweed
- ½ cup finely chopped fresh parsley
- 4 eggs
- ¾ teaspoon salt
- ⅛ teaspoon *each* freshly ground pepper and ground nutmeg
- ½ pound feta cheese, crumbled (about 1¾ cups)
- ½ pound (half of a 1-lb package) filo dough, thawed if frozen
- ¾ cup butter, melted

1. Remove and discard stems from spinach; you should have about 4 quarts leaves. Set spinach aside.

2. In a large frying pan cook onion and green onions in heated olive oil over medium heat until soft and golden. Remove with a slotted spoon and reserve. To oil in same pan add spinach, lifting and turning for 1 to 3 minutes just until leaves are wilted. Drain spinach well, pressing out moisture; chop coarsely. Add to onion mixture with dillweed and parsley.

3. In a large bowl beat eggs with salt, pepper, and nutmeg. Lightly mix in vegetable mixture and feta cheese.

4. Unfold sheets of filo dough so they lie flat. Cover with plastic wrap, then a damp towel, to prevent them from drying out. Brush a 9- by 13-inch pan generously with some of the melted butter. Line pan with 1 sheet of filo, brush with melted butter, and cover with 5 more sheets of filo, brushing each with melted butter and letting filo overlap sides of pan.

5. Pour in spinach mixture, spreading it evenly. Fold overhanging filo back over spinach. Top with remaining sheets of filo dough, each folded to fit pan and brushed with butter. Brush top with any remaining butter. Using a razor blade or small, sharp knife, cut through top layers of filo to mark 24 squares. (If made ahead, cover and refrigerate.)

6. Bake, uncovered, in a 350°F oven until pastry is well browned (45 minutes to 1 hour). Place pan on a rack to cool slightly, then finish cutting into squares, following the original cuts. Serve warm or at room temperature.

Makes 24 pieces (6 to 8 servings).

CHICKEN AND VEAL FILO ROLLS

Resembling individual pâtés, these walnut-accented nuggets are delicious for brunch with white wine, buttered carrots, and mixed sweet pickles. Precede them with a seasonal fresh fruit bowl.

- 2 whole chicken breasts (4 halves, about 2 lbs total), boned and skinned
- 1 small onion, finely chopped
- 2 tablespoons *each* butter or margarine and brandy
- 1 egg
- ¼ cup soft bread crumbs
- 1 teaspoon salt
- ⅛ teaspoon *each* white pepper and ground allspice
- 1 pound ground veal *or* turkey
- ¼ cup chopped fresh parsley
- ⅓ cup coarsely chopped toasted walnuts
- 12 sheets (about ½ lb) filo dough, thawed if frozen
- ½ cup butter or margarine, melted

1. Cut boned chicken breasts crosswise into ½-inch strips. Cook chicken strips and onion in the 2 tablespoons butter in a large frying pan, stirring often, over medium heat until lightly browned. Mix in brandy and cook, stirring, until most of the liquid is gone. Remove from heat.

2. In a large bowl beat egg slightly; mix in bread crumbs, salt, pepper, and allspice. Then lightly mix in veal, parsley, walnuts, and chicken mixture.

3. Unfold sheets of filo dough so they lie flat. Cover with plastic wrap, then a damp towel, to prevent them from drying out. Remove one sheet of filo at a time, brush half with melted butter, and fold in half to make a rectangle about 9 by 12 inches. Brush again with butter.

4. Shape about ⅓ cup of the chicken mixture into a roll and place at narrow end of dough. Fold in sides of filo about 1½ inches and roll up. Place seam side down on greased or nonstick baking sheets. Repeat for remaining dough and filling. (If made ahead, cover and refrigerate.) Brush with remaining butter.

5. Bake in a 350°F oven until golden brown (30 to 35 minutes). Serve hot.

Makes 12 rolls (6 servings).

FILLED LOAVES AND PASTRIES

Enclosing foods in a crust, or en croûte, *has become popular, and such baked brunch dishes can indeed make a handsome presentation. A buttery brioche dough, plain or whole wheat, leavened with yeast, is simpler to stir up and use as a wrapping than you might expect. Sheets of frozen puff pastry can also be employed to spectacular effect.*

PROVENÇAL TOMATO GALETTES

The French eat a *galette* (a sweet or savory filled turnover) as a snack or lunch, but you will find these delightful for brunch. Made with packaged puff pastry, they go together quickly. Accompany them with Elegant Oranges (see page 22) for a first course; then serve crisp raw vegetables —radishes, and carrot and cucumber sticks—on ice with the turnovers.

- 2 large onions, slivered
- ¼ cup olive oil
- 1 large can (28 oz) tomatoes
- ½ teaspoon *each* sugar, salt, and dried rosemary
- ⅛ teaspoon cayenne pepper
- 1 clove garlic, minced or pressed
- 1 cup julienne ham
- 1 package (17¼ oz) frozen puff pastry, thawed for 20 minutes
- 24 tiny Niçoise olives *or* halved, pitted ripe olives
- 1 egg, beaten with 1 teaspoon water

1. In a large frying pan cook onions in 2 tablespoons of the oil over medium heat, stirring occasionally, until soft and lightly browned. Remove with a slotted spoon and reserve.

2. Heat remaining 2 tablespoons oil in same pan. Add tomatoes (coarsely chopped) and their liquid, sugar, salt, rosemary, cayenne, and garlic. Cook over high heat, stirring occasionally, until mixture is thickened and reduced to about 2 cups. Mix in ham.

3. Roll each sheet of puff pastry out on a floured board or pastry cloth to a 12-inch square. Divide each piece of pastry into four 6-inch squares. On each square place an eighth of the onions and about ¼ cup of the tomato sauce. Top each with 3 olives. Bring opposite corners of each square to meet in center, pinching together in center and at edges to hold. Place on greased or nonstick baking sheets. Brush lightly with egg mixture.

4. Bake in a 450°F oven until pastry is well browned (15 to 18 minutes).

Makes 8 servings.

HOT PORK AND HAM PÂTÉ IN BRIOCHE

French through and through, this hot pâté is baked inside a buttery brioche dough. The tart little pickles called *cornichons* complement its garlic-accented flavor, as do creamed spinach and a sprightly young red wine such as a French Beaujolais.

Brioche Dough (recipe follows)
- 1 **large onion, finely chopped**
- 2 **tablespoons butter *or* margarine**
- 1 **clove garlic, minced *or* pressed**
- ¼ **cup brandy**
- 1 **egg**
- ⅛ **cup soft bread crumbs**
- 1 **pound ground pork**
- 2 **cups ground baked ham**
- ¼ **cup finely chopped fresh parsley**
- ½ **teaspoon *each* salt and dried thyme**
- ¼ **teaspoon ground allspice**
- ⅛ **teaspoon white pepper**
- 1 **egg, beaten with 1 teaspoon water**

1. Prepare Brioche Dough, and while it is rising, make filling.

2. Cook onion in butter until soft but not browned. Mix in garlic and brandy; cook, stirring, until most of the liquid cooks away.

3. Beat the 1 egg in a large bowl. Mix in bread crumbs, then ground meats, onion mixture, parsley, salt, thyme, allspice, and pepper. Cover and refrigerate until ready to enclose in dough.

4. Roll dough out on a generously floured board or pastry cloth to make a rectangle about 10 by 20 inches. Shape filling with your hands into a loaf about 4 by 8 inches. Place filling at one end of a narrow side of dough, about 1 inch in from end. Roll, jelly roll fashion, to other end of dough. Pinch dough to seal ends. Place, with long sealed edge at bottom, in a well greased 5- by 9-inch loaf pan.

5. Cover lightly with waxed paper and let rise in a warm place until dough looks puffy (about 30 minutes). Or, cover and refrigerate for several hours or overnight; remove from refrigerator about 1 hour (until puffy looking) before baking.

6. Brush lightly with beaten egg mixture. Bake in a 350°F oven until dough is well browned and juices run clear when a long skewer is inserted in center (about 1½ hours).

7. Place pâté (still in pan) on a rack and let stand for about 15 minutes; then carefully remove loaf from pan and cut into 1-inch-thick slices. Serve warm.

Makes 6 to 8 servings.

Brioche Dough: Sprinkle 1 package active dry yeast over ¼ cup warm water in large bowl of an electric mixer; let stand for 5 minutes to soften. Mix in 1 tablespoon sugar and ½ teaspoon salt, then ½ cup all-purpose flour. Beat at medium speed until elastic (about 3 minutes). Beat in 2 eggs, one at a time, until smooth, then gradually beat in 1½ cups all-purpose flour. Add ½ cup (¼ lb) butter or margarine (softened), 1 tablespoon at a time, beating well after each addition. Transfer to a greased bowl, cover, and let rise in a warm place until doubled (about 1½ hours). Stir dough down.

Brunch on the patio when the weather is fine, and for a French touch feature this Hot Pork and Ham Pâté in Brioche. It can be assembled in advance, then baked the day of the party to serve warm.

A honeyed wheat pastry encloses a ratatouille filling, baked in a spring-form pan and served warm.

RATATOUILLE IN A WHOLE WHEAT SHELL

Cut wedges of this vegetable-filled pastry, baked in a springform pan. Complement the robust red pepper and eggplant filling with grilled garlic sausages and a green salad.

Wheat Dough (recipe follows)
1 small eggplant (about 1 lb), cut in ½-inch (unpeeled) cubes
1 medium onion, slivered
¼ cup olive oil
½ pound mushrooms, thinly sliced
1 sweet red (or green) bell pepper, seeded and cut in strips
1 clove garlic, minced or pressed
¾ teaspoon *each* dried basil and oregano
½ teaspoon salt
⅛ teaspoon pepper
Pinch cayenne pepper
1 can (1 lb) tomatoes
2 eggs
¼ cup shredded Parmesan cheese
1 cup (4 oz) shredded Swiss cheese
1 egg, beaten with 1 teaspoon water

1. Prepare Wheat Dough, and while it is rising, make filling.

2. Cook eggplant and onion, stirring often, in heated oil in a large frying pan over medium heat until vegetables are soft (about 10 minutes). Add mushrooms and red pepper; cook, stirring occasionally, until mushrooms brown lightly. Mix in garlic, basil, oregano, salt, pepper, cayenne, and tomatoes (coarsely chopped) and their liquid.

3. Bring mixture to boiling, reduce heat, and simmer, stirring occasionally, until mixture is thick and reduced to about 4 cups (20 to 25 minutes). Remove from heat and let cool for about 10 minutes.

4. Beat the 2 eggs slightly in a medium bowl. Mix lightly into vegetable mixture with Parmesan and Swiss cheeses.

5. Using well-floured hands, shape about two-thirds of the dough into a ball. Roll out on a generously floured board or pastry cloth to about a 14-inch circle. Line a well-greased 8-inch springform pan with dough.

6. Spread vegetable mixture in dough-lined pan. Fold edge of dough down over edge of filling. Roll out remaining dough to a circle a little larger than the pan. Place over filling; moisten edges and press together with a fork to seal.

7. Cover lightly with waxed paper and let rise in a warm place until dough looks puffy (30 to 45 minutes).

8. Brush lightly with beaten egg mixture. Bake in a 375°F oven until dough is richly browned and sounds hollow when tapped (about 1 hour).

9. Let stand in pan on a rack for about 15 minutes before removing sides of pan. Cut in wedges and serve warm or at room temperature.

Makes 8 servings.

Wheat Dough: Sprinkle 1 package active dry yeast over ¼ cup warm water in large bowl of an electric mixer; let stand for 5 minutes to soften. Mix in 1 tablespoon honey and ½ teaspoon salt, then ½ cup all-purpose flour. Beat at medium speed until elastic (about 3 minutes). Beat in 2 eggs, one at a time, until smooth, then gradually beat in ½ cup whole wheat flour and 1 cup all-purpose flour. Add ½ cup (¼ lb) butter or margarine (softened), 1 tablespoon at a time, beating well after each addition. Transfer to a greased bowl, cover, and let rise in a warm place until doubled (about 1½ hours). Stir dough down.

BREAKFAST PIZZA

For a shortcut breakfast, these appealing individual pizzas are made on split English muffins. If you like, they can be assembled ahead and refrigerated, then baked quickly in the morning.

2 medium onions, finely chopped
2 tablespoons olive oil
1 clove garlic, minced or pressed
1 teaspoon dried oregano
6 English muffins, split
¼ pound thinly sliced coppa, capicolla, *or* ham, cut in thin strips
2 medium tomatoes
⅔ cup grated Parmesan cheese
2 cups shredded Monterey jack cheese

1. Cook onions in heated oil in a large frying pan over medium heat, stirring often, until soft and lightly browned. Mix in garlic and oregano; remove from heat and set aside.

2. Arrange English muffins on a baking sheet and broil until cut sides are browned. Divide onion mixture evenly over the 12 muffin halves, spreading it to edges. Then add a layer of coppa strips.

3. Cut each tomato crosswise into 6 slices. Place a tomato slice over meat strips on each muffin, then add layers of Parmesan and Monterey jack cheeses.

4. Bake pizzas in a 450°F oven for 10 to 15 minutes, until cheese is melted and lightly browned.

Makes 6 servings (2 pizzas each).

FRUIT TARTS

People who aren't expert pastry chefs sometimes avoid attempting sweet pies. But if you use a tender press-in pastry (plain or with ground nuts for part of its substance) for fruit pies, you will be pleasantly surprised by the quality of crust you can achieve without any special skills.

RHUBARB MERINGUE TART

Baked in a large, removable-bottom, round tart pan, this fresh rhubarb pie makes a handsome presentation for a spring brunch.

Press-In Pastry (recipe follows)
3 eggs, separated
1 cup sugar
2 tablespoons all-purpose flour
⅛ teaspoon ground nutmeg
½ teaspoon grated orange rind
¼ cup *each* orange juice and whipping cream
4 cups diced rhubarb
Meringue (recipe follows)

1. Press pastry into bottom and up the sides of an 11-inch removable-bottom tart pan.

2. Beat egg yolks and sugar until thick and pale; blend in flour, nutmeg, and orange rind, then orange juice and whipping cream. Fold in rhubarb, mixing lightly to coat. Spread in prepared pastry shell.

3. Bake in a 450°F oven for 10 minutes; reduce heat to 350°F and bake for 25 to 30 minutes, until filling is set and rhubarb is tender. Remove tart from oven.

4. Spread meringue lightly over rhubarb filling. Return to 350°F oven and bake until meringue is a pale golden brown (8 to 10 minutes).

5. Remove pan sides and serve tart warm or at room temperature.

Makes 1 pie (6 to 8 servings).

Press-In Pastry: Mix 1½ cups all-purpose flour with ¼ cup sugar. Cut in ½ cup (¼ lb) firm butter or margarine until crumbly. Beat 1 egg yolk with ½ teaspoon vanilla. With a fork, stir egg mixture lightly into flour mixture, then use your hands to press dough together into a smooth, flattened ball.

Meringue: Beat 3 egg whites (reserved from yolks used in filling) until frothy; beat in ⅛ teaspoon cream of tartar and continue beating until soft peaks form. Gradually add ¼ cup sugar, beating until mixture is stiff and glossy.

FRESH PLUM KUCHEN

Early autumn's fresh small blue prune plums bake to crimson juiciness in this sugar-sprinkled brunch dessert.

　　Press-In Pastry (see this page)
⅔ **cup sugar**
¼ **teaspoon ground nutmeg**
3 **tablespoons all-purpose flour**
1 **tablespoon lemon juice**
4 **cups (about 1½ lbs) small blue prune plums, halved and pitted**
1 **tablespoon butter or margarine**
　　Sugar
　　Sour cream

1. Press pastry into the bottom and about halfway up the sides of a 9-inch springform pan.

2. Mix sugar, nutmeg, and flour. Stir lemon juice into plums in a bowl, then mix lightly with sugar mixture. Arrange fruit, cut sides up, making 2 layers in pastry-lined pan. Sprinkle with any sugar mixture remaining in bowl. Dot with butter.

3. Bake on lowest rack of a 375°F oven for 50 minutes to 1 hour, until pastry is well browned and plums are tender and bubbling. Sprinkle lightly with sugar.

4. Remove pan sides and serve tart warm or cool with *Crème Fraîche* or sour cream spooned over each piece.

Makes 6 to 8 servings.

FRESH APRICOT TART

Wait for fresh apricot time to delight brunch guests with this almond-sprinkled fruit tart in a luscious pastry containing ground almonds.

　　Almond Press-In Pastry (recipe follows)
4 **cups halved, pitted apricots (about 2 lbs)**
⅓ **cup sugar**
1 **teaspoon cornstarch**
⅛ **teaspoon ground nutmeg**
2 **tablespoons butter or margarine**
⅔ **cup apricot preserves**
1 **tablespoon orange-flavored liqueur**
¼ **cup toasted sliced almonds**

1. Press pastry into bottom and up the sides of an 11-inch removable-bottom tart pan.

2. Arrange apricots, cut sides down and overlapping slightly, in pastry-lined pan. Mix sugar, cornstarch, and nutmeg; sprinkle over apricots. Dot with butter.

3. Bake in a 450°F oven for 12 minutes; reduce heat to 350°F and bake until apricots are tender and crust is brown (25 to 30 minutes). Cool in pan on a wire rack.

4. Heat preserves until melted and bubbling; strain to remove solid pieces of fruit. Mix in liqueur. Spoon glaze evenly over apricots. Sprinkle edge with sliced almonds to make about a 2-inch border.

5. Remove pan sides to serve tart at room temperature.

Makes 1 pie (6 to 8 servings).

Almond Press-In Pastry: Mix 1¼ cups all-purpose flour with ¼ cup *each* ground blanched almonds (whirled in blender or food processor until powdery) and sugar. Cut in ½ cup (¼ lb) firm butter or margarine until crumbly. Blend 1 egg yolk with ¼ teaspoon *each* vanilla and almond extract. With a fork, stir egg mixture lightly into flour mixture, then use your hands to press dough together into a smooth, flat ball.

There's no brunch dessert more appetizing than this Fresh Apricot Tart. It has an almond pastry shell.

The better the bread, the better the breakfast. Augment bakery bread with your own irresistible muffins, coffee cakes, loaves, and sweet rolls.

HOMEMADE BREAKFAST BREADS

Bread is the mainstay of any breakfast. When it is baked in your own kitchen, you can count on a warm, fragrant bread to coax slugabeds pleasantly to the breakfast table.

Although fresh-baked flavor and crusty-outside, moist-inside texture are strong reasons for the appeal of homemade breads, you need not always bake them quite that immediately—bread-baking being, in most instances, a rather drawn-out process.

Instead, you can bake breads at your convenience, freeze them while they are at their peak, then thaw and reheat them days or weeks later to dazzle family and friends at breakfast or brunch.

The selection in this chapter includes both quick breads (muffins, scones, popovers, fruit-and-nut breads, and easy coffee cakes) and breads with the distinctive flavor and springy texture yeast contributes. In this group you will find wheaty whole grain loaves, an elegant braided egg bread, uncomplicated beaten-batter breads, *croissants,* and some tempting sweet rolls.

Top them all off with a selection of homemade jams and preserves, sealing in the goodness of fresh spring and summer fruits. They will enhance your lovingly created breads at the breakfast table all year long.

Welcome the morning with a basket of warm, freshly baked Apple-Pecan Muffins; the recipe is on page 84. If made ahead, they can be frozen and reheated.

QUICK BREADS

The designation quick bread *includes muffins, fruit and nut breads, and easy coffee cakes. What they have in common is a leavening of baking powder or baking soda. That means that these breads can be stirred together in a few minutes and baked at once, without the lengthy rising period yeast breads need.*

MINIATURE CINNAMON MUFFINS

Cakelike in texture, these delicate currant-studded muffins are dunked while warm from the oven in butter and cinnamon-sugar. Snugly wrapped to stay warm, they are an irresistible feature of a brunch buffet.

These cinnamon-sugared muffins are tiny two-bite-sized temptations. Serve them warm for brunch.

1½ cups all-purpose flour
1½ teaspoons baking powder
¼ teaspoon *each* salt and ground nutmeg
¼ cup dried currants
⅓ cup butter or margarine, softened
½ cup sugar
½ teaspoon vanilla
1 egg
½ cup milk
6 tablespoons butter or margarine, melted
Cinnamon-Sugar (recipe follows)

1. In a medium bowl mix flour, baking powder, salt, nutmeg, and currants.

2. In large mixer bowl cream the ⅓ cup butter with sugar, then beat in vanilla and egg until well combined. Add flour mixture to butter mixture alternately with milk, mixing after each addition just until combined.

3. Fill greased 1¾-inch muffin pans two-thirds full.

4. Bake in a 375°F oven until muffins are golden brown (18 to 20 minutes). Remove hot muffins from pans at once and dip quickly into the melted butter, then roll in Cinnamon-Sugar to coat. Serve warm.

Makes 2 dozen 1¾-inch muffins.

Cinnamon-Sugar: In a small bowl thoroughly combine ½ cup sugar and 1 teaspoon ground cinnamon.

ORANGE MARMALADE MUFFINS

Muffins are one of the fastest quick breads, and with only a little planning, you can stir up a batch even on a weekday morning. They consist of a dry and a liquid mixture. To prepare for speedy assembly, mix the dry ingredients in one bowl, the liquid in another. (Refrigerate liquid mixture if done more than an hour ahead.)

Have muffin pans greased and ready to use. Then quickly combine the two mixtures, and spoon the batter into the pans. In less than half an hour the muffins will be ready to eat, temptingly hot.

This recipe also includes three variations: savory cheese muffins with sesame seeds, moist apple and pecan muffins, and tart fresh cranberry muffins with spices.

- **2 cups all-purpose flour**
- **¼ cup sugar**
- **1 tablespoon baking powder**
- **½ teaspoon salt**
- **1 egg**
- **1 cup milk**
- **3 tablespoons butter or margarine (melted) or salad oil**
- **2 teaspoons grated orange rind**
- **⅓ cup orange marmalade**

1. In a large bowl stir together flour, sugar, baking powder, and salt.

2. In a medium bowl beat egg with milk, melted butter, and orange rind. Add egg mixture to flour mixture, stirring only until flour is moistened.

3. Fill greased 2½-inch muffin pans a third full. To each, add about 1 teaspoon of marmalade. Use remaining batter to fill pans two-thirds full.

4. Bake in a 400°F oven until muffins are well browned (20 to 25 minutes). Serve warm.

Makes 1 dozen muffins.

Cheddar Cheese Muffins. Omit orange rind and marmalade. Decrease sugar to 2 tablespoons. To flour mixture add 1 cup shredded Cheddar cheese. After filling greased muffin pans two-thirds full with cheese batter, sprinkle muffins lightly with sesame seeds, using about 2 teaspoons in all.

Apple-Pecan Muffins. Omit orange rind and marmalade. Increase sugar to ⅓ cup. To flour mixture add ½ teaspoon ground cinnamon and ¼ cup finely chopped pecans. To egg mixture add 1 small tart apple (peeled, cored, and shredded). Using a total of ¼ cup finely chopped pecans, sprinkle each muffin lightly with pecans before baking, using about 1 teaspoon for each. Increase baking time to a total of 25 to 30 minutes.

Spiced Cranberry Muffins. Omit orange marmalade. Coarsely chop ¾ cup fresh cranberries; measure ½ cup sugar, and mix ⅓ cup of it into cranberries in a small bowl. Let stand while preparing muffin batter. In flour mixture use the remaining measured sugar (2 tablespoons plus 2 teaspoons) in place of the ¼ cup called for in basic recipe. To flour mixture add ½ teaspoon ground cinnamon and ¼ teaspoon ground nutmeg. After adding the egg mixture to the flour mixture, stir in cranberry mixture with last few strokes. Increase baking time to a total of 25 to 30 minutes.

ORANGE-DATE MUFFINS

Moist and dense with chopped fresh orange, walnuts, and dates, these muffins have a deliciously fresh flavor.

- **1 small orange**
- **1 cup all-purpose flour**
- **¼ teaspoon each salt and baking powder**
- **½ teaspoon baking soda**
- **¾ teaspoon ground cinnamon**
- **½ cup finely chopped walnuts**
- **⅓ cup chopped dates**
- **1 egg**
- **½ cup firmly packed brown sugar**
- **⅓ cup salad oil**
- **½ teaspoon vanilla**

1. Grate and reserve rind from orange. Then cut off and discard any remaining rind and all white membrane from orange. Finely chop orange (discard seeds if any) and add grated rind. Measure and add orange juice, if necessary, to make ⅔ cup.

2. Mix flour, salt, baking powder, baking soda, cinnamon, walnuts, and dates in a large bowl. In a medium bowl beat egg with brown sugar and oil until blended. Mix in vanilla and orange mixture.

3. Add egg mixture to flour mixture, stirring only until flour is moistened. Divide batter into greased 2½-inch muffin pans.

4. Bake in a 375°F oven for 20 to 25 minutes, until muffins are well browned and a wooden pick inserted in centers comes out clean. Serve warm or at room temperature.

Makes 1 dozen muffins.

MAPLE-NUT BRAN MUFFINS

These layered bran muffins include a luxurious touch — real maple sugar in the cinnamon-walnut filling. If it is not available, you can substitute brown sugar.

- **1 cup whole-bran cereal**
- **¾ cup milk**
- **1 egg**
- **¼ cup soft shortening**
- **1 cup all-purpose flour**
- **2½ teaspoons baking powder**
- **½ teaspoon salt**
- **¼ cup sugar**
  Maple-Nut Filling (recipe follows)

1. In a medium bowl combine cereal and milk; let stand until most of the liquid is absorbed. Beat in egg and shortening.

2. In a large bowl mix flour, baking powder, salt, and sugar. Add cereal mixture, mixing only until combined.

3. Spoon a small amount of batter into each of 12 greased or nonstick 2½-inch muffin pans; sprinkle with some of the filling. Repeat layers until pans are about three-fourths full.

4. Bake in a 400°F oven for 20 to 25 minutes, until muffins are well browned. Serve warm.

Makes 1 dozen muffins.

Maple-Nut Filling: Mix ½ cup packed maple sugar, ½ cup finely chopped walnuts, 2 tablespoons flour, and ½ teaspoon ground cinnamon.

AUNTIE'S SCONES

A scone (it rhymes with gone) is a sweet, buttery biscuit with a British background. Buttermilk makes these remarkably crisp crusted, yet moist within.

- **2 cups all-purpose flour**
- **1 teaspoon cream of tartar**
- **½ teaspoon baking soda**
- **⅛ teaspoon salt**
- **¼ cup sugar**
- **½ cup firm butter or margarine**
- **¼ to ⅓ cup buttermilk**
  Warm Honey Butter (recipe follows)

1. In a medium bowl stir together flour, cream of tartar, baking soda, salt, and sugar. Cut in butter until mixture is uniformly crumbly and the consistency of coarse crumbs.

2. Gradually stir in buttermilk, 1 tablespoon at a time, just until mixture is moist enough to cling together. (Too much mixing or too much liquid will make the scones tough.)

3. With floured hands, lightly shape dough into a flattened ball. Roll out on a floured board or pastry cloth to a circle about 8 inches in diameter and ½ inch thick. Using a floured 2½-inch cutter, cut into rounds. Place on a greased or nonstick baking sheet.

4. Bake in a 350°F oven until golden brown (15 to 20 minutes).

5. Serve warm, split and drizzled with warm Honey Butter.

Makes 10 to 12 scones.

Honey Butter: In a small pan over medium heat combine ¼ cup each butter or margarine and honey, stirring until blended and hot. Makes about ½ cup.

CRISPY POPOVERS

A popover is a stunning quick bread —billowing and crusty. A successfully executed popover is nearly all outside, with a perfectly hollow interior. That means it has lots of space to fill with butter and jam, or something as substantial as creamed poultry or seafood.

This recipe has a handy feature. The batter can be made ahead in your blender or food processor, then refrigerated for hours or overnight before baking. For success, avoid opening the oven until popovers are nearly at the end of their baking time.

- **1 cup milk**
- **2 eggs**
- **1 tablespoon butter, melted or salad oil**
- **1 cup all-purpose flour**
- **¼ teaspoon salt**
- **1 tablespoon sugar**

1. Preheat oven to 400°F. Generously butter 2½-inch muffin or popover pans.

2. In blender or food processor combine milk, eggs, butter, flour, salt, and sugar. Whirl until smooth and well combined, stopping motor and scraping flour from sides of container once or twice. (If made ahead, cover and refrigerate. Stir batter well before using.) Pour batter into prepared pans, filling them about half full.

3. Bake (avoid opening oven during baking) until popovers are well browned and firm to the touch (35 to 40 minutes). Serve hot.

Makes 10 to 12 popovers.

TOASTED COCONUT BANANA BREAD

A generous measure of coconut lends a tropical flavor to this favorite fruit-nut bread.

- **1 cup flaked coconut**
- **2 cups all-purpose flour**
- **1 tablespoon baking powder**
- **1 teaspoon ground cinnamon**
- **½ teaspoon each salt and baking soda**
- **¾ cup sugar**
- **1 cup finely chopped walnuts**
- **1 egg**
- **¼ cup milk**
- **⅓ cup salad oil**
- **1 teaspoon vanilla**
- **2 soft-ripe bananas**

1. Spread coconut in a shallow pan and bake in a 350°F oven, stirring occasionally, until lightly toasted (12 to 15 minutes). Set aside to cool.

2. In a large bowl mix flour, baking powder, cinnamon, salt, baking soda, and sugar. Stir in walnuts and coconut.

3. Beat egg with milk, salad oil, and vanilla until well combined. Mash bananas (you should have about 1 cup); blend with egg

mixture. Add banana mixture to dry ingredients, mixing just until blended.

4. Spread in a greased, lightly floured 4½- by 8½-inch loaf pan.

5. Bake in a 350°F oven until loaf is well browned and a wooden pick inserted in center comes out clean (50 to 60 minutes). Let stand 10 minutes, then turn out onto a wire rack to cool completely. Flavor is best if, after cooling, bread is wrapped and allowed to stand at least 1 day.

Makes 1 loaf.

SOUR CREAM COFFEE RING

Baked in a bundt or other fancy tube pan, this wheaty coffeecake makes a dramatic presentation. As you cut each slice, you'll see a swirled layer of the spicy nut filling.

- **2 cups all-purpose flour**
- **1 cup whole wheat flour**
- **¾ teaspoon baking soda**
- **1 tablespoon baking powder**
- **½ teaspoon salt**
- **¾ cup butter or margarine, softened**
- **1 cup granulated sugar**
- **½ cup firmly packed brown sugar**
- **1 teaspoon vanilla**
- **3 eggs**
- **1½ cups sour cream**
  Cinnamon-Walnut Filling (recipe follows)
- **2 tablespoons firm butter or margarine, cut in pieces**
  Powdered sugar

1. Stir together flours, soda, baking powder, and salt.

2. In a large bowl cream the ¾ cup butter with granulated and brown sugars until light and fluffy. Blend in vanilla. Then add eggs, one at a time, beating well after each addition.

3. Add flour mixture to creamed mixture alternately with sour cream, mixing to blend after each addition.

4. Spoon about 2 tablespoons of the Cinnamon-Walnut Filling over bottom of a well greased, lightly floured 10-inch bundt or other tube pan with a capacity of 10 to 12 cups. Spoon in half of the batter. Sprinkle evenly with about half of the remaining filling; dot with 1 tablespoon of the firm butter. Add remaining batter, then sprinkle with remaining filling, and dot with remaining butter.

5. Bake in a 350°F oven until cake tests done when a long skewer is inserted in thickest part (45 to 50 minutes).

6. Let stand in pan on a wire rack for about 10 minutes, then invert out of pan. Dust with powdered sugar before serving.

Makes 1 coffeecake (8 to 10 servings.).

Cinnamon-Walnut Filling: In a small bowl mix ½ cup sugar, 1½ teaspoons ground cinnamon, and ½ cup finely chopped walnuts.

A layer of spiced walnuts swirls through the center of this powdered sugar-dusted Sour Cream Coffee Ring.

BLUEBERRY COFFEE CAKE

Dust powdered sugar over this almond-crusted fresh blueberry cake to dramatize its luscious looks.

- ¼ **cup *each* sliced almonds and firmly packed brown sugar**
- 1½ **cups all-purpose flour**
- ¾ **cup granulated sugar**
- 1 **tablespoon baking powder**
- ½ **teaspoon salt**
- ¼ **teaspoon ground nutmeg**
- ⅓ **cup butter or margarine**
- 1 **cup fresh blueberries**
- 1 **egg**
- ½ **cup milk**
- 1 **teaspoon vanilla**
  Powdered sugar

1. Generously grease a 9-inch tube pan with a capacity of 6 to 7 cups. Sprinkle with mixture of almonds and brown sugar; set aside.

2. In a bowl mix flour, granulated sugar, baking powder, salt, and nutmeg; cut in butter until mixture resembles coarse crumbs. Lightly stir in blueberries.

3. In a small bowl beat egg lightly with milk and vanilla. Stir milk mixture into blueberry mixture just until combined. Spread batter gently in prepared pan.

4. Bake in a 350°F oven until coffee cake is well browned and a long skewer inserted in thickest part comes out clean (45 minutes to 1 hour).

5. Let stand in pan for about 5 minutes, loosen edges, and invert onto a serving plate. Serve warm or at room temperature, dusted with powdered sugar.

Makes 1 coffee cake.

BANANA-NUT COFFEE CAKE

A crumbly brown sugar and walnut mixture tops this spicy, orange-accented banana cake.

- ¼ **cup butter or margarine, softened**
- ⅓ **cup sugar**
- 1 **soft-ripe banana, mashed (about ½ cup)**
- ¼ **cup sour cream**
- 1 **egg**
- 2 **teaspoons grated orange rind**
- 1¼ **cups all-purpose flour**
- 1 **tablespoon baking powder**
- ½ **teaspoon baking soda**
- ¼ **teaspoon *each* salt and ground nutmeg**
- ¼ **cup milk**
  Brown Sugar Streusel (recipe follows)
- ⅓ **cup chopped walnuts**

1. In a large bowl cream butter and sugar until fluffy; blend in banana, sour cream, egg, and orange rind.

2. Mix flour, baking powder, soda, salt, and nutmeg. Stir flour mixture into banana mixture alternately with milk, blending after each addition just until combined. Spread in a greased 8-inch-square baking pan.

3. Sprinkle evenly with Brown Sugar Streusel, then with walnuts.

4. Bake in a 375°F oven until pick inserted in center comes out clean (35 to 40 minutes). Let cool slightly before cutting into squares. Serve warm or at room temperature.

Makes 1 coffee cake.

Brown Sugar Streusel: In a small bowl mix ¼ cup *each* all-purpose flour and firmly packed brown sugar, 2 tablespoons granulated sugar, and ½ teaspoon ground cinnamon. Cut in 3 tablespoons firm butter or margarine until coarse crumbs form.

CINNAMON COFFEE CAKE "PIE"

Vinegar adds a fruity tang to the flavor of this oldtime breakfast bread, sweetened, in part, with honey. Baked in an 8-inch-round cake pan, the coffee cake is just the right size for a weekend morning treat for the family.

- 1½ **cups all-purpose flour**
- ¾ **teaspoon *each* baking soda and ground cinnamon**
- ½ **teaspoon salt**
- ⅓ **cup butter or margarine, softened**
- ¼ **cup sugar**
- ½ **cup honey**
- 1 **teaspoon vanilla**
- 2 **eggs**
- 3 **tablespoons white vinegar**
  Powdered Sugar Topping (recipe follows)

1. Stir together flour, soda, cinnamon, and salt.

2. In a large bowl cream butter and sugar until fluffy. Blend in honey and vanilla. Then add eggs, one at a time, beating well after each addition.

3. Add flour mixture to creamed mixture alternately with vinegar, mixing to blend after each addition. Spread batter in a greased, lightly floured 8-inch-round cake pan. Sprinkle evenly with Powdered Sugar Topping.

4. Bake in a 375°F oven until pick inserted in center comes out clean (25 to 30 minutes). Cut in wedges and serve warm.

Makes 1 coffee cake.

Powdered Sugar Topping: In a small bowl mix 2 tablespoons powdered sugar and ½ teaspoon ground cinnamon until well combined.

Almond-crusted Blueberry Coffee Cake is inviting for breakfast, served warm or at room temperature.

CARAMEL-TOPPED OATMEAL BREAKFAST CAKE

A broiled brown sugar and nut topping gilds this moist, spicy breakfast cake. Squares of it are delicious with tea.

- 1¼ cups boiling water
- 1 cup rolled oats
- ½ cup raisins
- ½ cup butter or margarine, softened
- 1 cup granulated sugar
- 1 cup firmly packed brown sugar
- 1 teaspoon vanilla
- 2 eggs
- 1½ cups all-purpose flour
- 1 teaspoon baking soda
- ¾ teaspoon ground cinnamon
- ½ teaspoon salt
- ¼ teaspoon ground nutmeg
- Caramel Topping (recipe follows)

1. Pour boiling water over oats and raisins in a medium bowl; let stand until lukewarm.

2. In a large bowl cream butter with sugars until light and fluffy. Blend in vanilla. Then add eggs, one at a time, beating well after each addition. Blend in oatmeal mixture.

3. Stir together flour, soda, cinnamon, salt, and nutmeg. Blend flour mixture into oatmeal mixture. Spread batter in a well-greased, lightly floured 9-inch-square baking pan.

4. Bake in a 350°F oven until top of cake springs back when touched lightly (45 to 50 minutes).

5. Spread lightly with Caramel Topping. Broil, about 4 inches from heat, until topping browns and bubbles (about 2 minutes). Let cool slightly, then cut into squares.

Makes 1 coffee cake (10 to 12 servings).

Caramel Topping: In a small pan melt ¼ cup butter or margarine. Remove from heat and mix in ½ cup firmly packed brown sugar, 2 tablespoons half-and-half (light cream), and 1 cup finely chopped walnuts.

LEMON DROP TEACAKE

Lots of fresh lemon flavors this pretty, syrup-soaked ground almond cake. Inside, it is also moist with yogurt.

- 1 cup butter *or* margarine, softened
- 1 cup sugar
- 1½ teaspoons grated lemon rind
- 1 teaspoon vanilla
- 4 eggs (at room temperature)
- 2½ cups all-purpose flour
- 1 teaspoon *each* baking powder and baking soda
- ¼ teaspoon salt
- 1 cup finely ground blanched almonds (whirled in blender or food processor until powdery)
- 1 cup plain yogurt
- Lemon Syrup (recipe follows)

1. In a large bowl cream butter and sugar until fluffy. Beat in lemon rind and vanilla, then add eggs, one at a time, beating well after each addition.

2. Mix flour, baking powder, soda, salt, and almonds. Add flour mixture to butter mixture alternately with yogurt, beating well after each addition.

3. Pour batter into a well-greased, lightly floured 8½- to 9-inch bundt pan or other 9-cup tube pan.

4. Bake in a 350°F oven for 50 to 60 minutes, until cake pulls away from sides of pan and tests done when a long skewer is inserted in thickest part. Using a fork, pierce surface of cake all over. Slowly pour Lemon Syrup over hot cake. Let cake cool in pan on a wire rack.

5. Invert cake onto a plate to cut and serve.

Makes 1 cake (8 to 10 servings).

Lemon Syrup: In a small saucepan stir ½ cup sugar, ⅓ cup lemon juice, and 2 tablespoons water over medium heat until sugar dissolves and mixture boils. Boil for 2 minutes. Keep warm until ready to use.

YEAST BREADS

Breads leavened with yeast take more time, work, and attention than do quick breads. But to those who enjoy creating—and eating —such breads, the rewards surpass the effort. Here is a sampling of yeast breads with special morning appeal.

EASY BATTER BRIOCHES

Here are eggy, golden rolls to complement almost any brunch main dish—or to serve simply with butter and jam.

- 2 packages active dry yeast
- ¼ cup warm water
- ½ cup warm milk
- ⅔ cup butter or margarine
- ¼ cup sugar
- ½ teaspoon salt
- 3¾ to 4 cups all-purpose flour
- 4 eggs

1. Sprinkle yeast over warm water in large electric mixer bowl. Let stand until soft (about 5 minutes). Add warm milk, butter, sugar, and salt; stir until butter melts.

2. Blend in 2 cups of the flour; beat at medium speed for 3 minutes. Add eggs, one at a time, beating well after each addition. Gradually beat in 1¾ to 2 cups additional flour to make a stiff batter, beating until batter is smooth (3 to 5 minutes).

3. Transfer batter to a greased bowl, cover, and let rise in a warm place until bubbly (about 1 hour). Stir batter down,

then divide it equally into well-greased 2½- inch muffin pans, filling them about two-thirds full.

4. Let rise until doubled (20 to 25 minutes).

5. Bake in a 350°F oven until well browned (20 to 25 minutes). Let stand in pans for a few minutes, then remove to wire racks to cool.

Makes 18 rolls.

HONEY-WHEAT TOASTING BREAD

If peanut butter with toast is your idea of a wonderful morning combination, try it on this bread some day for breakfast. The dense, intensely flavorful bread is also fine with plum or other homemade preserves.

- 2 packages active dry yeast
- ½ cup warm water
- 2 cups warm milk
- ½ cup honey
- 2 tablespoons salad oil
- 2 teaspoons salt
- 3 cups whole wheat flour
- 3½ to 4 cups all-purpose flour
- 1 cup wheat germ

1. Sprinkle yeast over warm water in large bowl of an electric mixer; let stand until soft (about 5 minutes). Stir in milk, honey, oil, salt, whole wheat flour, and 2 cups of the all-purpose flour. Mix to blend, then beat at medium speed until smooth and elastic (about 5 minutes).

2. Mix in wheat germ and about 1½ cups of the all-purpose flour to make a moderately stiff dough. Turn out on a board or pastry cloth floured with some of the remaining ½ cup all-purpose flour. Knead until dough is elastic and small bubbles form just beneath surface (about 10 minutes).

3. Turn dough in a greased bowl. Cover and let rise in a warm place until doubled (1 to 1½ hours). Punch dough down, divide into two equal parts, and let rest 10 minutes. Shape into two loaves and place in greased 4½- by 8½-inch baking pans. Cover lightly and let rise until loaves fill pans to tops (30 to 45 minutes).

4. Bake in a 375°F oven until loaves are well browned and sound hollow when tapped (30 to 35 minutes). Turn out onto racks to cool before slicing and toasting.

Makes 2 loaves.

ITALIAN SAUSAGE BREAD

Crumbled sausage flavors this round, wheat-flecked loaf, a specialty of Italian bakers in New Jersey. Made ahead and reheated, it complements a brunch of tomato juice or Bloody Marys, scrambled eggs, and a cheese such as Fontina or Monterey jack sliced from a big wedge.

- **1 package active dry yeast**
- **¼ cup warm water**
- **1 cup warm milk**
- **1 tablespoon sugar**
- **½ teaspoon salt**
- **2 tablespoons olive oil**
- **3 to 3¼ cups all-purpose flour**
- **½ cup whole wheat flour**
- **½ pound mild Italian sausages**
- **1 egg yolk, beaten with 1 teaspoon water**

1. Sprinkle yeast over warm water in large electric mixer bowl. Let stand until soft (about 5 minutes). Stir in milk, sugar, salt, and 1 tablespoon of the oil.

2. Add 2½ cups of the all-purpose flour. Mix to blend, then beat at medium speed until smooth and elastic (about 5 minutes). Stir in whole wheat flour and about ¼ cup more all-purpose flour to make a stiff dough.

3. Turn dough out onto a board or pastry cloth floured with some of the remaining ¼ to ½ cup flour. Knead until dough is smooth and satiny and small bubbles form just under surface, adding more flour to prevent dough from being too sticky (about 15 minutes).

4. Turn dough in a greased bowl. Cover and let rise in a warm place until doubled (45 minutes to 1 hour). Meanwhile, remove casings from sausages and crumble meat. Brown lightly, stirring often, in a medium frying pan over moderate heat. Remove with a slotted spoon and drain and cool on paper towels. Punch risen dough down and pat into a ½-inch-thick circle.

5. Sprinkle sausage over round of dough. Knead and fold lightly into dough, then shape it into a ball. Pat out to a round 8 inches in diameter. Place on a greased baking sheet. With a 3¼-inch-round cutter or empty tuna can, cut a circle in center, leaving round of dough in place.

6. Brush dough with remaining 1 tablespoon oil. Let rise until puffy (30 to 45 minutes). Brush with egg yolk mixture.

7. Bake in a 375°F oven until crust is a rich golden brown and loaf sounds hollow when tapped (25 to 30 minutes). Cool slightly on a rack before slicing. Cut in wedges to serve.

Makes 1 large loaf.

FILBERT LOAVES

Toasted filberts—some call them hazelnuts—perfume these rich little loaves. The bread is delicious spread with the rich, creamy Italian cheese called *mascarpone*.

This recipe makes two small loaves, so you can serve one now and freeze the other. Or you can also bake the bread in a single 5- by 9-inch loaf pan, allowing longer for the larger loaf to rise and bake.

- **¾ cup filberts**
- **1 package active dry yeast**
- **¼ cup warm water**
- **½ cup warm milk**
- **¼ cup sugar**
- **½ teaspoon *each* salt, vanilla, and grated lemon rind**
- **2 tablespoons butter or margarine**
- **3 to 3¼ cups all-purpose flour**
- **2 eggs**
- **1 teaspoon water**
- **1 tablespoon sugar**

1. Spread filberts in a shallow pan. Bake in a 350°F oven until lightly browned (8 to 10 minutes). Cool slightly, then chop coarsely.

2. Sprinkle yeast over warm water in large electric mixer bowl. Let stand until soft (about 5 minutes). Add warm milk, the ¼ cup sugar, salt, vanilla, lemon rind, and butter. Stir until butter melts.

3. Add 1½ cups of the flour. Mix to blend, then beat at medium speed until smooth and elastic (about 5 minutes). Beat in 1 whole egg and egg yolk (reserve egg white for glaze), then ½ cup of the filberts. Gradually stir in about 1¼ cups more flour to make a soft dough.

4. Turn dough out onto a board or pastry cloth floured with some of the remaining ¼ to ½ cup flour. Knead until dough is smooth and satiny and small bubbles form just under surface, adding more flour to prevent dough from being too sticky (about 15 minutes).

5. Turn dough in a greased bowl. Cover and let rise in a warm place until doubled (1¼ to 1½ hours). Punch dough down and divide it into 2 equal portions.

6. Sprinkle 2 greased small loaf pans (about 3½ by 7½ inches) lightly with some of the remaining chopped filberts, using about 1 tablespoon for each pan. Shape each half of dough into a loaf. Place in prepared pans. Let rise until almost doubled (about 45 minutes). Slightly beat reserved egg white with the 1 teaspoon water; brush mixture lightly over loaves. Sprinkle with remaining filberts and the 1 tablespoon sugar. (Use 1½ teaspoons sugar for each loaf.)

7. Bake in a 375°F oven until well browned (25 to 30 minutes).

Makes 2 small loaves.

BRAIDED EGG BREAD

Nothing exceeds the pride a baker feels at opening the oven to see a grand, spectacularly puffed loaf of braided egg bread, such as this traditional *challah*. The crust is speckled with sesame or poppy seeds.

- **1 package active dry yeast**
- **1¼ cups warm water**
- **2 teaspoons sugar**
- **1 teaspoon salt**
- **2 tablespoons salad oil**
- **4½ to 5 cups all-purpose flour**
- **2 eggs**
- **1 egg yolk, beaten with ½ teaspoon water**
- **3 tablespoons sesame seeds or poppy seeds**

1. Sprinkle yeast over ¼ cup of the warm water in large electric mixer bowl. Let stand until soft (about 5 minutes). Add remaining 1 cup warm water, sugar, salt, and oil.

2. Add 3 cups of the flour. Mix to blend, then beat at medium speed until smooth and elastic (about 5 minutes). Beat in eggs, one at a time, then gradually stir in about 1½ cups more flour to make a soft dough.

3. Turn dough out onto a board or pastry cloth floured with some of the remaining ½ cup flour. Knead until dough is smooth and satiny and small bubbles form just under surface, adding more flour to prevent dough from being too sticky (about 15 minutes).

4. Turn dough in a greased bowl. Cover and let rise in a warm place until doubled (about 1 hour). Punch down, cover again, and let rise a second time until doubled (about 45 minutes). Punch dough down and divide it into 3 equal portions.

5. On a lightly floured surface roll each portion to an 18-inch-long strand. Place the 3 strands side by side diagonally across a greased baking sheet; braid. Pinch ends to seal. Let rise until almost doubled (about 45 minutes). Brush egg yolk mixture lightly over braid. Sprinkle evenly with sesame seeds or poppy seeds.

6. Bake in a 375°F oven until braid is well browned and sounds hollow when tapped lightly (40 to 45 minutes).

Makes 1 large loaf.

These four yeast breads can be the star of the breakfast—or brunch—table. Clockwise from upper left: Honey-Wheat Toasting Bread (recipe on page 87), Braided Egg Bread, Italian Sausage Bread, and Filbert Loaves.

SWISS CHRISTMAS BREAKFAST

Oranges
Swiss Almond Fruit Loaves
Butter
Soft-Cooked Eggs
Hot Chocolate *or* Coffee

Here is a holiday morning breakfast to enjoy in stages. Amid the excitement of emptying the Christmas stockings and unwrapping the packages beneath the tree, munch orange sections and sip chocolate or coffee.

Wrap the previously baked loaves in foil to warm, then cook eggs when the hubbub subsides. (They take only 3 to 5 minutes; see page 29.)

SWISS ALMOND FRUIT LOAVES

- 2 packages active dry yeast
- ½ cup warm water
- 1 cup warm milk
- ¼ cup butter or margarine, softened
- ¼ cup sugar
- 1 teaspoon *each* salt and ground mace *or* nutmeg
- 4½ to 5 cups all-purpose flour
- 1 egg
- ½ cup *each* raisins, slivered almonds, and diced mixed candied fruits
- 2 tablespoons egg white, slightly beaten
- 2 tablespoons Vanilla Sugar (see page 22)

1. Sprinkle yeast over warm water in large electric mixer bowl. Let stand until soft (about 5 minutes). Add milk, butter, sugar, salt, and mace; stir until butter melts.

2. Add 3 cups of the flour. Mix to blend, then beat until smooth and elastic (about 5 minutes). Beat in egg. Stir in about 1 cup more flour to make a soft dough. Mix in raisins, almonds, and candied fruits.

3. Turn dough out on a board or pastry cloth floured with some of the remaining ½ to 1 cup flour; knead until dough is smooth, springy, and develops small bubbles just under the surface (15 to 20 minutes).

4. Turn dough in a greased bowl. Cover and let rise in a warm place until doubled (about 1 hour). Punch dough down. Turn out on a floured surface and knead lightly to expel air bubbles. Divide into 2 equal parts.

5. Shape each half of the dough into a loaf. Place in generously greased 4½- by 8½-inch loaf pans.

6. Let rise until dough just reaches tops of pans (30 to 45 minutes). Brush tops of loaves lightly with beaten egg white. Sprinkle evenly with Vanilla Sugar.

7. Bake in a 375°F oven until loaves are well browned and sound hollow when tapped (30 to 35 minutes). Carefully remove from pans and let loaves cool on wire racks.

Makes 2 loaves.

ORANGE BUNDT BATTER BREAD

Beating the batter for this simple yeast bread until it is so elastic that it pulls away from the side of the bowl is important. It gives the tender orange bread a light, almost cakelike texture. Drizzled with orange icing and decorated with chopped almonds, it is a festive holiday choice.

      2 **packages active dry yeast**
    ¼ **cup warm water**
    ½ **cup warm milk**
    ⅓ **cup sugar**
    ¾ **teaspoon salt**
    ⅔ **cup butter or margarine, softened**
    1½ **teaspoons vanilla**
      4 **eggs**
      1 **teaspoon grated orange rind**
      4 **cups all-purpose flour**
        Orange Glaze (recipe follows)
        Chopped toasted almonds, for garnish

1. Sprinkle yeast over warm water in large bowl of an electric mixer; let stand until soft (about 5 minutes). Add warm milk, sugar, salt, and butter; stir until butter melts. Mix in vanilla, eggs, and orange rind, beating until well combined.

2. Add flour, 1 cup at a time, beating well after each addition. When all the flour has been added, beat at medium speed until batter is elastic (3 to 5 minutes).

3. Transfer batter to a greased bowl. Cover and let rise in a warm place until bubbly (about 1 hour). Stir down; spread batter in a well-greased 10-inch tube pan, bundt pan, or other fancy 10 to 12-cup mold. Let rise until doubled (about 45 minutes).

4. Bake in a 350°F oven for 30 to 35 minutes, until well browned.

5. Invert bread from pan onto a wire rack to cool. While still warm, drizzle with Orange Glaze and decorate with almonds.

Makes 1 large coffeecake.

Orange Glaze: In a small bowl combine 1 cup powdered sugar, 2 teaspoons butter or margarine (softened), ½ teaspoon grated orange rind, and 2 tablespoons orange juice. Mix until smooth.

CROISSANTS

Crisp, flaky, butter in every crumb—croissants are the essence of the Continental breakfast. More and more bakers are turning out croissants that rival those made in France. If you are willing to spend the time, so can you.

   This is one recipe that calls for butter and butter alone; margarine just doesn't produce the same flavor or crisply layered texture. If you are going to take the trouble to make croissants, it is worth using the best ingredients.

      1 **package active dry yeast**
    ¼ **cup warm water**
    ¾ **cup warm milk**
      1 **tablespoon sugar**
    ¼ **teaspoon salt**
      1 **tablespoon butter, softened**
    2¾ **cups all-purpose flour**
      1 **cup butter, softened**
      1 **egg yolk, beaten with 1 teaspoon water**

1. Sprinkle yeast over warm water in large electric mixer bowl. Let stand until soft (about 5 minutes). Add warm milk, sugar, salt, and the 1 tablespoon butter, stirring until butter melts.

2. Add 1¼ cups of the flour. Mix to blend, then beat at medium speed until smooth (about 3 minutes). Mix in about 1 cup more flour to make a soft dough.

3. Turn out on board or pastry cloth floured with the remaining ½ cup flour. Turn dough in flour to coat well. Knead gently until flour is incorporated.

4. Turn dough in greased bowl. Cover and let rise in a warm place until doubled (45 minutes to 1 hour). Punch down, cover, and refrigerate for at least 1 hour (or as long as several hours or overnight if you wish).

5. Roll dough out to a rectangle about ¼ inch thick. Using a fourth of the 1 cup butter (it should be just soft enough to spread, but not melting), spread it over center third of the dough.

6. Fold sides of dough over buttered center, sealing edges. Again roll dough out to a ¼-inch-thick rectangle. Spread center third with another fourth of the butter, then repeat folding and sealing. Wrap dough in plastic film and refrigerate for 30 minutes.

7. Again roll dough to a ¼-inch-thick rectangle, spread with another fourth of the butter, fold, and seal. If dough is soft, wrap and refrigerate for another 30 minutes; otherwise, continue. Then complete dough by rolling to a ¼-inch-thick rectangle, spread center third with last fourth of the butter, and fold and seal as before. Wrap again and refrigerate until firm (1 hour or longer).

8. Divide dough in half. (Wrap and return half to refrigerator.) Roll each portion of dough out on floured surface to a 13-inch-diameter circle. Cut each circle into 6 equal triangles. Starting from wide end of each, roll toward point. Place each roll with point on underside on ungreased baking sheet, curving ends to make a crescent shape.

9. Cover lightly with plastic wrap and let rise at room temperature until nearly doubled (45 minutes to 1 hour). Brush lightly with egg yolk mixture.

10. Bake in a 400°F oven for 10 minutes; reduce heat to 350°F and bake until croissants are golden brown (18 to 20 minutes).

Makes 12 rolls.

CROISSANT TIPS

Croissants derive their flakiness from layers of butter worked into the chilled dough in stages, as described in the first two steps.

Roll chilled dough out to a rectangle, then spread ¼ cup softened butter over center third of it.

Fold unspread thirds of the dough from both sides to cover buttered center. Seal edges, then chill dough before adding another portion of butter. Repeat three more times until all the butter is incorporated.

Each half of chilled dough is rolled out to a 13-inch-diameter circle, then cut into 6 equal triangles.

Starting from wide end, roll each triangle of croissant dough gently but firmly toward point. Curve into a crescent and place on baking sheet with points underneath.

CINNAMON-RAISIN BUNS

Wheat germ in the dough makes these coiled raisin rolls seem both nutlike in flavor and somehow healthy. They are a cozy accompaniment to a mid-morning cup of breakfast tea or spicy herbal tea.

    2 packages active dry yeast
 1¾ cups warm water
  ⅓ cup sugar
    1 teaspoon salt
    3 tablespoons salad oil
 4½ to 5 cups all-purpose flour
  ⅓ cup wheat germ
  ⅓ cup firm butter or margarine,
       thinly sliced
       Cinnamon-Sugar (recipe
       follows)
  ½ cup raisins
       Egg White Glaze (recipe follows)
       Powdered Sugar Frosting
       (recipe follows)

1. In large bowl of an electric mixer sprinkle yeast over water; let stand until softened (about 5 minutes). Mix in sugar, salt, and oil. Stir in 3 cups of the flour, then beat at medium speed until mixture is elastic and pulls away from sides of bowl (about 5 minutes).

2. Stir in wheat germ and about 1½ cups more flour to make a soft dough. Turn out on a board or pastry cloth sprinkled with some of the remaining ½ cup flour. Knead until dough is smooth and satiny and small bubbles form beneath surface, kneading in additional flour as needed if dough seems sticky (15 to 20 minutes).

3. Place dough in a greased bowl, turning to coat all sides. Cover and let rise in a warm place until doubled in bulk (about 1 hour).

4. Punch dough down. Roll out on a floured surface to a 12- by 18-inch rectangle. Cover evenly with butter slices, then sprinkle with Cinnamon-Sugar. Sprinkle evenly with raisins. Starting from a long end, roll dough up, jelly-roll fashion. Moisten and pinch edge to seal. Cut into 12 equal slices.

5. Place slices, cut sides down, in a well-greased 10- by 15-inch baking pan. Cover with waxed paper and let rise until rolls are puffy (25 to 30 minutes). Brush lightly with Egg White Glaze.

6. Bake in a 400°F oven until well browned (20 to 25 minutes). Serve warm or at room temperature, drizzled with Powdered Sugar Frosting.

Makes 12 rolls.

Cinnamon-Sugar: In a small bowl mix ½ cup sugar and 1 tablespoon ground cinnamon.

Egg White Glaze: In a small bowl beat 1 egg white with 1 teaspoon water and ½ teaspoon sugar until slightly foamy.

Powdered Sugar Frosting: Place ¾ cup powdered sugar in a small bowl. Add ½ teaspoon vanilla and 1½ to 2 tablespoons warm water, mixing until smooth and creamy.

BAKED NUTMEG DOUGHNUTS

Although these doughnut-shaped rolls are baked, not fried, they resemble a doughnut in flavor. The dough requires no kneading and is light and puffy in texture.

    2 packages active dry yeast
  ¼ cup warm water
 1⅓ cups warm milk
  ¼ cup sugar
    1 teaspoon salt
    2 teaspoons ground nutmeg
  ¼ teaspoon ground cinnamon
  ⅔ cup butter or margarine
 4½ to 5 cups all-purpose flour
    2 eggs
  ½ cup Vanilla Sugar (see page 22)

1. Sprinkle yeast over warm water in large electric mixer bowl. Let stand until soft (about 5 minutes). Add warm milk, the ¼ cup sugar, salt, nutmeg, cinnamon, and ⅓ cup of the butter; stir until butter melts.

2. Add 3 cups of the flour. Mix to blend, then beat at medium speed until smooth and elastic (about 5 minutes). Beat in eggs, then gradually stir in about 1½ cups more flour to make a soft dough.

3. Transfer to a greased bowl, cover, and let rise in a warm place until doubled (about 1 hour). Stir dough down.

4. Turn dough out on a well floured board or pastry cloth (use some of the remaining ½ cup flour) and shape with floured hands into a flattened ball; coat well with flour. Lightly roll out about ½ inch thick. Cut with a floured 2½-inch doughnut cutter. Place doughnuts about 2 inches apart on greased baking sheets.

5. Brush lightly with some of the remaining ⅓ cup butter, melted, and let rise until nearly doubled (about 30 minutes).

6. Bake in a 425°F oven until doughnuts are golden brown (about 10 minutes). Brush warm doughnuts with remaining melted butter and roll lightly in Vanilla Sugar.

Makes 3 dozen doughnuts.

To brighten up a drizzly gray morning, serve a breakfast of warm, homemade Cinnamon Raisin Buns and cups of cheering tea.

HONEY-NUT CRESCENTS

Rolled, crescentlike, from wedges of sour cream dough, these fruit-filled tidbits (some call them *rugalach*) are something of a breakfast cookie.

1 package active dry yeast
¼ cup warm water
2½ cups all-purpose flour
½ teaspoon salt
½ cup (¼ lb) butter or margarine
2 eggs, separated
½ teaspoon vanilla
½ cup sour cream
Powdered sugar
¼ cup honey
½ cup raisins
⅔ cup chopped walnuts
¼ cup granulated sugar, mixed with ½ teaspoon ground cinnamon
2 teaspoons water

1. In a medium bowl sprinkle yeast over the ¼ cup warm water and let stand until soft (about 5 minutes).

2. In large electric mixer bowl stir together flour and salt. Cut in butter until mixture resembles coarse crumbs. To yeast mixture add egg yolks (reserve whites for glaze), vanilla, and sour cream; beat until blended. Gradually add yeast mixture to flour mixture, mixing until flour is moistened. Turn dough out onto a floured board or pastry cloth and knead just until smooth; shape dough into a flattened ball.

3. Wrap dough in plastic film and refrigerate for several hours or overnight.

4. Divide dough in half. Roll each half out to a 12-inch-diameter round on board or pastry cloth sprinkled lightly with powdered sugar. Warm honey slightly to make it easier to spread. Brush each round of dough with half of the honey, then sprinkle with half *each* of the raisins, walnuts, and cinnamon-sugar mixture.

5. Cut each round into 12 equal triangles. Starting at a wide end, roll each wedge toward point. Place, points down, about 2 inches apart on greased baking sheets. Curve ends slightly to make a crescent shape.

6. Cover crescents lightly with waxed paper and let stand in a warm place until puffy looking (20 to 25 minutes). Beat reserved 2 egg whites with the 2 teaspoons water. Brush crescents lightly with egg white mixture.

7. Bake in a 350°F oven until rolls are richly browned (18 to 20 minutes).

Makes 2 dozen rolls.

Brunch, Italian-style: Jam-Filled Crescents and a Bellini—an apéritif that combines fresh peaches and sparkling wine (the recipe is on page 18).

ITALIAN JAM-FILLED CRESCENTS

Shaped like crescents, these rolls have a much more tender, brioche-like texture than flaky French croissants. Each reveals a center of apricot preserves.

2 packages active dry yeast
½ cup warm water
¾ cup warm milk
¾ cup granulated sugar
1 teaspoon *each* salt and vanilla
½ cup butter or margarine, softened
5½ to 6 cups all-purpose flour
3 eggs
½ cup apricot preserves *or* orange marmalade
2 teaspoons water
Pearl sugar *or* coarsely crushed sugar cubes

1. Sprinkle yeast over warm water in large electric mixer bowl. Let stand until soft (about 5 minutes). Add warm milk, granulated sugar, salt, vanilla, and butter; stir until butter melts.

2. Add 3 cups of the flour. Mix to blend, then beat at medium speed until smooth and elastic (about 5 minutes). Beat in 1 whole egg and 2 egg yolks (reserve egg whites for glaze), then gradually stir in 2 to 2½ cups more flour to make a soft dough.

3. Turn dough out onto a board or pastry cloth floured with some of the remaining ½ to 1 cup flour. Knead until dough is smooth and satiny and small bubbles form just under surface, adding more flour to prevent dough from being too sticky (about 15 minutes).

4. Turn dough in a greased bowl. Cover and let rise in a warm place until doubled (about 1½ hours). Punch dough down, divide it into 2 equal portions, and let stand for 10 minutes.

5. Roll each portion of dough out on a floured surface to an 18-inch-diameter circle. Cut each round into 12 equal triangles. Place about 1 teaspoon apricot preserves at wide end of each triangle. Starting from wide end of each, roll toward point. Place each roll on a greased baking sheet with point on underside, curving ends slightly to make a crescent shape.

6. Cover lightly and let rolls rise until puffy looking (25 to 30 minutes). Beat reserved 2 egg whites with the 2 teaspoons water. Brush egg white mixture lightly over rolls. Sprinkle lightly with pearl sugar.

7. Bake in a 375°F oven until well browned (15 to 20 minutes).

Makes 2 dozen rolls.

FOR YOUR HOMEMADE BREAD, FOUR CHOICE JAMS

Nothing tastes better with homemade bread than homemade jam or preserves. Take advantage of fresh spring and summer fruits to put up some of these delicious spreads. Each is a fairly small recipe and can be made without preparing a vast quantity of fruit.

SWEET CHERRY CONSERVE

- **4 cups Bing cherries, stemmed and pitted**
- **3 cups sugar**
- **2 tablespoons lemon juice**
- **¼ teaspoon salt**
- **½ cup slivered almonds**

1. In a large, heavy saucepan (3-quart or larger capacity) combine cherries, sugar, lemon juice, and salt. Bring to boiling over medium heat, stirring until sugar dissolves.

2. Increase heat to medium-high and boil, uncovered, stirring often, until mixture begins to thicken and sheets from a spoon (about 15 minutes). Stir in almonds and bring again to boiling.

3. Pour hot conserve into hot sterilized jars and seal as directed on this page.

Makes about 3 cups (half-pints).

STRAWBERRY-RHUBARB PRESERVES

- **3 cups firm-ripe strawberries, hulled**
- **2 cups diced rhubarb**
- **5 cups sugar**
- **¼ cup lemon juice**

1. In a large bowl combine berries, rhubarb, and sugar. Cover and refrigerate for 8 hours or overnight.

2. Transfer mixture to a large, heavy saucepan, place over medium-high heat, and bring to a full rolling boil. Boil for 8 minutes.

3. Add lemon juice, bring again to boiling, and boil for 3 minutes more.

4. Pour hot preserves into hot sterilized jars and seal as directed on this page.

Makes about 5 cups (half-pints).

SPICED NECTARINE BUTTER

- **4 pounds nectarines (about 10 large)**
- **1 cup water**
- **2 tablespoons lemon juice**
- **¼ teaspoon salt**
- **1 teaspoon ground cinnamon**
- **¼ teaspoon *each* ground cloves and nutmeg**
- **2½ cups firmly packed brown sugar**

1. Halve and pit (but do not peel) nectarines. Place in a large, deep, heavy saucepan with water and lemon juice. Cover and bring to a gentle boil over medium heat. Cook until nectarines are tender when pierced (15 to 20 minutes).

2. Transfer mixture, about half at a time, to a food processor or blender and process or whirl until smooth.

3. Return to cooking pan and add salt, spices, and brown sugar. Cook, uncovered, over medium-low heat, stirring occasionally and adjusting heat so mixture boils gently, until nectarine butter is thick and reduced to 5 to 6 cups. As mixture thickens, stir often. Allow 1 to 1¼ hours for cooking.

4. Pour hot nectarine butter into hot sterilized jars and seal as directed on this page.

Makes 5 to 6 cups (half-pints).

OLD-FASHIONED BLUEBERRY JAM

- **6 cups blueberries**
- **3 cups sugar**
- **3 tablespoons lemon juice**
- **¼ teaspoon ground nutmeg**
- **½ teaspoon ground cinnamon**

1. In a large bowl combine berries, sugar, lemon juice, and spices. Crush berries slightly. Cover, refrigerate, and let stand for 8 hours or overnight.

2. Transfer mixture to a large, heavy saucepan, place over medium-high heat, and bring to a full rolling boil, stirring until sugar dissolves.

3. Reduce heat so jam boils gently and cook, stirring occasionally, until jam thickens slightly and sheets from a spoon (15 to 20 minutes).

4. Pour hot jam into hot sterilized jars and seal as directed on this page.

Makes about 4 cups (half-pints).

Packing and Sealing Jams and Preserves

The best way of preserving jams and jellies for long-term storage to insure safety and goodness is to pack them in standard canning jars with self-sealing lids and rims.

1. First sterilize the jars. Place them in a large pan in enough water to cover. Bring water to a vigorous boil. Reduce heat and let jars stand in simmering water until you are ready to use them (15 minutes or longer).

2. Just before filling jars, remove them with tongs and invert them on several thicknesses of clean kitchen towels. Scald lids and rims in boiling water.

3. Filling one jar at a time, pour hot jam or other preserves into hot sterilized jars. Wipe the rim at once with a clean, damp cloth. Put lid and rim in place, tightening the rim by hand. Quickly tip the jar upside down, then turn it right side up again. Place on a rack or board to cool. Repeat with remaining jars.

4. As the preserves cool, you may hear a series of pops; each of these signals that a jar has sealed. When cool, check jars for a good seal. When you press down on each lid, the center should feel slightly concave and stay down after you remove your finger. Any jars that have not sealed should be stored in the refrigerator.

A Tip for Jellymakers

Undercooked jam or jelly with be runny; if overcooked, it will be rubbery. How to know when just the right stage is reached? It can be a tricky judgment, depending on ripeness of fruit and cooking temperature.

To test jelly or jam for doneness, dip a cool metal spoon into the boiling liquid. Lift the spoon out and tip it so jelly runs off the edge. When the jelly falls in two drops and then flows together to form a sheet, it is ready.

U.S. MEASURE AND METRIC MEASURE CONVERSION CHART

Formulas for Exact Measures	Symbol	When you know:	Multiply by:	To find:	Rounded Measures for Quick Reference		
Mass (Weight)	oz	ounces	28.35	grams	1 oz	=2 tbsp	=30 g
	lb	pounds	0.45	kilograms	4 oz	=1/2 c	=115 g
	g	grams	0.035	ounces	8 oz	=1c	=225 g
	kg	kilograms	2.2	pounds	16 oz	=1 lb	=450 g
					32 oz	=2 lb	=900 g
					36 oz	=2-1/4 lb	=1000g (1 k)
Volume	tsp	teaspoons	5.	milliliters	1/4 tsp	=1/24 oz	=1 ml
	tbsp	tablespoons	15.	milliliters	1/2 tsp	=1/12 oz	=2 ml
	fl oz	fluid ounces	29.57	milliliters	1 tsp	=1/6 oz	=5 ml
	c	cups	0.24	liters	1 tbsp	=1/2 oz	=15 ml
	pt	pints	0.47	liters	1 c	=8 oz	=250 ml
	qt	quarts	0.95	liters	2 c (1 pt)	=16 oz	=500 ml
	gal	gallons	3.785	liters	4 c (1 qt)	=32 oz	=1 l
	ml	milliliters	0.034	fluid ounces	4 qt (1 gal)	=128 oz	=3-3/4 l
Length	in	inches	2.54	centimeters	3/8 in	=1 cm	
	ft	feet	30.48	centimeters	1 in.	=2.5 cm	
	yd	yards	0.9144	meters	2 in.	=5 cm	
	mi	miles	1.609	kilometers	2-1/2 in.	=6.5 cm	
	km	kilometers	0.621	miles	12 in. (1 ft)	=30 cm	
	m	meters	1.094	yards	1 yd	=90 cm	
	cm	centimeters	0.39	inches	100 ft	=30 m	
					1 mi	=1.6 km	
Temperature	°F	Fahrenheit	5/9 (after subtracting 32)	Celsius	32°F	=0°C	
	°C	Celsius	9/5 (then add 32)	Fahrenheit	68°F	=20°C	
					212°F	=100°C	
Area	$in.^2$	square inches	6.452	square centimeters	$1 in.^2$	$=6.5 cm^2$	
	ft^2	square feet	929.	square centimeters	$1 ft^2$	$=930 cm^2$	
	yd^2	square yards	8361.	square centimeters	$1 yd^2$	$=8360 cm^2$	
	a	acres	4047.	square meters	1 a	$=4050 m^2$	